SOVEREIGN WEALTH FUNDS AND INTERNATIONAL POLITICAL ECONOMY

Global Finance Series

Edited by
John Kirton, Univeristy of Toronto, Canada,
Michele Fratianni, Indiana University, United States and
Paolo Savona, University of Rome Guglielmo Marconi, Italy

The intensifying globalization of the twenty-first century has brought a myriad of new managerial and political challenges for governing international finance. The return of synchronous global slowdown, mounting developed country debt, and new economy volatility have overturned established economic certainties. Proliferating financial crises, transnational terrorism, currency consolidation, and increasing demands that international finance should better serve public goods such as social and environmental security have all arisen to compound the problem.

The new public and private international institutions that are emerging to govern global finance have only just begun to comprehend and respond to this new world. Embracing international financial flows and foreign direct investment, in both the private and public sector dimensions, this series focuses on the challenges and opportunities faced by firms, national governments, and international institutions, and their roles in creating a new system of global finance.

Also in the series

Debt Relief Initiatives
Policy Design and Outcomes
Marco Arnone and Andrea F. Presbitero
ISBN 978-0-7546-7742-0

Making Global Economic Governance Effective
Hard and Soft Law Institutions in a Crowded World
Edited by John Kirton,
Marina Larionova and Paolo Savona
ISBN 978-0-7546-7671-3

G8 against Transnational Organized Crime
Amandine Scherrer
ISBN 978-0-7546-7544-0

Full series listing at the back of the book

Sovereign Wealth Funds and International Political Economy

MANDA SHEMIRANI
Old Dominion University, USA

Routledge
Taylor & Francis Group

LONDON AND NEW YORK

First published 2011 by Ashgate Publishing

2 Park Square, Milton Park, Abingdon, Oxon OX14 4RN
711 Third Avenue, New York, NY 10017, USA

Routledge is an imprint of the Taylor & Francis Group, an informa business

First issued in paperback 2016

British Library Cataloguing in Publication Data
Shemirani, Manda.
  Sovereign wealth funds and international political economy.
  – (Global finance series)
  1. Sovereign wealth funds. 2. Sovereign wealth funds–Case
  studies. 3. International economic relations. 4. Statens
  pensjonsfond-Utland. 5. ADIA. 6. Temasek Holdings.
  7. Investments, Russian.
  I. Title II. Series
  332.6'7252–dc22

Library of Congress Cataloging-in-Publication Data
Shemirani, Manda.
  Sovereign wealth funds and international political economy / by Manda Shemirani.
    p. cm. — (Global finance)
  Includes index.
  ISBN 978-1-4094-2207-5 (hardback) 1. Sovereign wealth funds.
  2. Investments, Foreign. 3. International finance. 4. International cooperation.
  5. Economics. I. Title.
  HJ3801.S54 2010
  332.67'312—dc22

2010048573

ISBN 978-1-4094-2207-5 (hbk)
ISBN 978-1-138-26116-7 (pbk)

Contents

To my parents

List of Figures

List of Tables

Preface

Over the past few years, the study of state–owned investment funds known as sovereign wealth funds (SWFs), with their diversified and international portfolios, has gained momentum. Interestingly, though many of these SWFs have existed for several decades, separately from the national or official reserves, their ventures and operations have only recently become an object of interest to other states. This political scrutiny of sovereign wealth funds' foreign investment, much of it stemming from political debates in the United States concerning the attempts by foreign entities to acquire stakes in US entities in 2005 and 2006, has centered on a question that has attracted considerable attention, especially in the United States and, to a lesser extent, Europe: Do SWFs pose a threat to recipient countries with respect to sovereignty, national security, or financial stability?

Although this question has been frequently raised, it did not represent the best approach to achieving an understanding of the underlying motives of these funds. In order to best understand the agenda and decision–making processes of SWFs and thereby be in a better position to predict their behavior, we should instead focus on the more fundamental questions of why SWFs were created in the first place, what their various goals are, and how the owner states balance these goals.

Another problem in the relatively new literature on SWFs has been that, oftentimes, researchers and analysts in both the economic and political camps have grouped all states that own SWFs into a single set and treated them as a whole, with little or no consideration given to their various individual traits. As the case studies in this book will show, owner states of SWFs are often diverse in regard to their political and economic structure, and, thus, their funds' agenda. Additionally, a SWF may pursue multiple goals simultaneously, and its agenda may be modified as the state's priorities or the environment in which it is functioning change.

The ultimate questions one might ask are, why have states established sovereign funds and what do investor states seek to accomplish? Through their portfolio diversification and international investment, SWFs may pursue varying goals, such as meeting future public pension obligations, insulating the domestic economy from international market volatility, and achieving a more efficient management of national financial assets.

By providing a systematic methodology for a micro–level study of SWFs that views these funds within a larger economic and political context, this book addresses shortcomings in the existing literature. The juxtaposition of economic and political perspectives allows us to study these funds from two important angles, while the examination of each fund independently sheds light on the distinctive characteristics of each fund.

Recognizing the varying characteristics and, therefore, the varying agendas, of SWFs, as well as the diversity of the systems of political economy among the owner states, has an important implication for both economic and political policy making: decision–making processes based solely on either political or economic considerations are often inefficient since they often fail to account for important benefits of SWF investments. The politically–based decisions discount the potential economic benefits that a SWF investment may have on the host economy. For instance, SWFs can provide long–term liquidity when short–term liquidity is tight and markets are contracting. SWFs can also contribute to greater market efficiency and lower volatility by diversifying the global investor base. At the same time, policy prescriptions based solely on financial grounds can overlook the potential political implications of SWF investments.

Fortunately, there is a whole host of literature in international political economy in which one can study the SWFs objectives. There are a number of schools of thought on the question of why a sovereign state would choose to establish a fund and engage in portfolio management and international investment. This book employs three alternative theoretical perspectives, drawn from major political economic theories, to explain the goals investor states may pursue through their SWFs.

The book also addresses shortcomings in the literature by proposing a systematic methodology for the micro–level study of these funds and subsequently applying it to four major SWFs. This research reveals that the dominant conception, which is that investor states are in pursuit of political power over other states, is unjustified. The assertion that SWFs are primarily used for balance of payments corrections is equally unsound. None of the funds were shown to have been used in order to exert political power over another state and none provided funding only to correct the balance of payments. Some states act as economic agents or entrepreneurs in order to increase the value of their assets. For others, accumulating the resources required for domestic compensation is the immediate goal.

We should also be aware that investments by SWFs create interdependencies between the investor and the recipient states. A critical and yet hardly–discussed issue is that vulnerabilities exist on both sides of these interdependent relationships. This means investor states, too, are exposed to various risks.

The idea of this book came to me at the height of the political debates over the motivations of sovereign wealth funds. Having a background in both international economics and political economy, I was troubled by the fact that the conclusions reached by the decision–makers were often based on political ideology rather than an impartial and holistic cost–benefit analysis. On many occasions, as the politicians argued heatedly, essential points were missed: that a purely political approach with respect to SWFs' international investments—an inherently economic activity—is misguided, and that the potential negative impacts on (or costs to) the recipient states should be reviewed in close conjunction with the potential economic benefits of SWF investments.

In the course of this research I have accumulated many debts. My largest intellectual debt is owed to David C. Earnest and Kurt Taylor Gaubatz for their comments and insights from both the economics and political science worlds. I am also thankful to Simon Serfaty, whose advice solidified my decision to go ahead with this topic and Larry Filer for his valuable comments. I am grateful to the participants at the 2009 International Studies Association–South Conference, where an early draft of this book was recognized as one of the best papers. I received many helpful suggestions and a great deal of encouragement for publishing my work.

Additionally, I would like to thank Nick Wilson for his superb editing skills and feedback on the original draft, and the editors and reviewers at Ashgate Publishing for their comments and support. I am also indebted to Svetoslav Georgiev for reading and editing the entire manuscript, his participation in critical discussions that we had all through the course of the research, and above all his patience and constant support. Finally, I am grateful to my parents for their encouragement. Needless to say, any errors that may remain are my own.

Chapter 1
Introduction

In late 2005 and early 2006, Sovereign Wealth Funds (SWFs)—some of which had been in existence since the 1950s—fell under the media spotlight for the first time. Policy makers in the states that were recipients of SWFs' investments became concerned about the underlying motivation of these funds, mainly because politicians and academics understood neither the fundamental reasons for the creation of SWFs nor the functioning of SWFs. A major concern for many recipient states of sovereign money was the "possibility that some SWFs might be used for overt or tacit political purposes."[1] To assess the validity of recipient states' concerns with respect to SWFs' investments, we first need to study how investor states employ these funds.

While there is no universally accepted definition of a Sovereign Wealth Fund, various financial institutions, government agencies, and international organizations have provided definitions that generally share three main characteristics: ownership by sovereign governments, management of portfolios other than official national reserves, and involvement in overseas investments. The definition of SWFs in this book combines all three of these characteristics but also incorporates an additional criterion—the absence of a monetary or fiscal regulatory function. That means that, for instance, Saudi Arabia Monetary Authority (SAMA) is excluded from the SWF pool since it performs a function similar to that of a central bank.

In the United States and some European countries, the political scrutiny of SWFs' overseas investments over the past few years was intensified due to the lack of information about these funds. More importantly, the politicians' mindset, which had been influenced by major historical events, was not open to the idea of government–owned funds making overseas investments. The dominant realist view that the state's main goal is the pursuit of power, and the resulting presumption that any investment by sovereign states is a means to exert political influence over the recipient state, resulted in the rejection of foreign ownership or the withdrawal of foreign investment proposals in the United States.

Interestingly, there was very little interest in SWFs and their investments until a Chinese government–owned company placed a bid to buy an American oil company in 2005, and later a government–owned company from the United Arab Emirates acquired a British company whose assets included six port facilities in the United States. In August 2005, the China National Offshore Oil Corporation (CNOOC) abandoned its initial $18.5 billion cash bid—a more attractive proposal than

---

1   Benjamin J. Cohen, "Sovereign Wealth Funds and National Security: The Great Tradeoff," *International Affairs* 85, no. 4 (2009): 713.

Chevron's—for Unocal when it was faced with political opposition in the United States Congress while the proposal was still under the review by the Committee on Foreign Investment in the United States (CFIUS). Dubai Ports World (DP World), which had acquired Peninsular and Oriental Steam Navigation Company (P&O), was also made to sell the port facilities to a United States–controlled firm under the pressure of widespread and intense congressional opposition, despite prior approval of the ownership change by the CFIUS.[2]

What these entities shared in their relationship with the United States was general skepticism and disapproval by the American policy makers. China, with its massive balance of payments surplus, artificially weak exchange rate, and various political issues, receives extra attention and scrutiny, as do the states in the Middle East for their oil and gas policies, positions with regard to regional conflicts, and their potential ties to the events of 9/11. Consequently, the investment by these states has been excessively politicized. The political controversy over foreign investment by Chinese and Emirati entities in 2005 and 2006 soon evolved into a major presumption among policy makers in the United States. National security rhetoric was used for the purpose of opposing investments by states of which the politicians did not approve. The presumption, subsequently, shifted the attention to SWFs that had been managing states' assets for decades without causing any concerns.

The problem is that protectionist policies in the recipient states—which may result from the politicization of foreign governments' investment—can trigger counter measures by investor states. Once their entry into the market of a potential recipient state is blocked, the investor states may decide to retaliate by blocking the entry of companies or capital flows from the protectionist states. In the end, the retributory actions by both investor and recipient states could undermine the long–fought–for global economic openness and put the foundation of the "free markets" at risk.

Decision–making processes, based solely on a political rationale, are not efficient. In other words, politically–based decisions discount the importance of potential economic benefits. In the case of states that are recipients of SWF investments, the potential gain from the inflow of foreign investment is often times overlooked. This is not to say that investment by sovereign states should be viewed in exactly the same way as investment by private entities; however, it should be considered with more objectivity. To be sure, dealing with SWFs and their investments is more complicated than dealing with private investors for two reasons. First, ownership by the governments makes it difficult to readily apply conventional economic theories to SWFs' investments. In other words, private sector economics may not be a suitable framework for the study of SWFs. Second,

---

2   Gary Clyde Hufbauer, Yee Wong, and Ketki Sheth, *US–China Trade Disputes: Rising Tide, Rising Stakes*, Policy Analyses in International Economics 78 (Peterson Institute for International Economics, 2006).

the economic nature of the investment itself makes the application of political or international relations theories to these funds more difficult.

The point—often missed in the heated debates among politicians—is that a purely political approach alone is misguided. Potential negative impacts on (or costs to) the recipient states should be reviewed in close conjunction with the potential economic benefits of SWF investments. The point is that in this kind of interdependent relationship, recipient states do not necessarily lose. SWFs can provide long term liquidity when short term liquidity is tight and markets are contracting. SWFs could also contribute to greater market efficiency and lower volatility by diversifying the global investor base.[3]

Investor states have various perspectives with respect to their sovereign funds. The opportunity cost of holding official reserves or excess capital in risk–free or fixed–income assets is continuously increasing, not only because of global inflation and downward pressures on the dollar—the unit of account for the majority of investor states—but also because of uncertainties such as the risk of natural disasters, conflicts, wars, and market turmoil. To reiterate, viewing the capital inflow from investor states—which has been mostly in the form of portfolio investment rather than direct investment—through a highly political lens can limit both our understanding of the true nature and purpose of the SWFs, as well as potential gains (economic and otherwise) from sovereign investments.

Another important issue is that the SWFs are not identical, i.e., their characteristics vary widely. As this book will show, the national system of political economy of the investor states influences the SWFs' motives and purposes. The multiplicity of forms and motives will be discussed in further details, but for now suffice it to say that the existence of such diversity among SWFs makes the application of a single policy ineffective. Policy prescriptions based on general— and perhaps inaccurate—assumptions about investor states can lead to over– and under–estimation of various risks.

In order to address these complications, an original and innovative theoretical approach, one that brings a new perspective to the political economy literature, is needed. This book presents a methodology for a micro–level analysis of SWFs, and proposes ways to distinguish the various motives of the investor states. In this book, I propose an answer to the question of whether recipient states should be concerned about the investments by SWFs. I have observed that the investment decisions and strategies of the four cases of SWFs examined here are based on certain fundamental yet uncomplicated principles other than the pursuit of power. The current research refutes the two mainstream conceptions of SWFs: (1) the policy makers' belief that these funds are a means of economic statecraft or foreign policy tool, aimed at exerting power over another state, and (2) the view of some economists that the role of these funds is limited to the correction of balance of payments deficit or monetary imbalances.

---

3   "Sovereign Wealth Funds–a Work Agenda," (International Monetary Fund, 2008), 12-3.

In fact, all of the investor states examined in this book (Norway, United Arab Emirates, Singapore and the Russian Federation) had a balance of payments surplus during most of the life of their funds. In addition to that, there was no evidence indicating that the investor states had ever used their funds in order to exercise power over any of the states in which they had made investments. Even in the case of the fund of Norway, whose investment decisions are often guided by a set of non–commercial guidelines, the targets were corporations, rather than the recipient states directly. Norway has certainly communicated its intentions to foreign states (e.g., Burma), but has done so without attempting to directly influence the government in the recipient state. This is what I call "benign economic statecraft."

States like United Arab Emirates and Singapore are far too small, and at the same time, preoccupied with their internal concerns, one being increasing the value of their assets. SWFs in these countries have acted mainly as an entrepreneurial arm of the state. On the other hand, various internal centers of power in Russia struggle to get access to the fund's assets. The main thrust of this book is that there are alternative political economic theories that suggest a more meaningful explanation for the creation, evolution, and functioning of SWFs than the pure economic or realist perspectives.

This book makes a number of important arguments. First, SWFs' management and operations reflect—to borrow Gilpin's term—the national system of political economy[4] as well as the political mindset of the leadership, which have been shaped by historical events. The multiplicity of political economic systems suggests a variety of SWF motives and purposes. Therefore, the one–size–fits–all approach to policy making with respect to these funds is not appropriate. In practice, as the study shows, the only time SWFs tend to show a similar behavior is at times of financial crisis, or severe economic contraction. The recent global financial crisis and economic downturn in countries around the world provided an excellent opportunity for testing this hypothesis, where its timing and extent of impact with respect to the various states was consistent.

Second, the management and operation of SWFs are not a static percept but a dynamic process; learning and adjustment are natural and inevitable. States also undergo changes over time as a result of changes in modes of production, demography, political system, technological advancements, and global forces. All these mean investor states and their sovereign funds have to be studied longitudinally.

And lastly, the lack of transparency is certainly an important issue, and a legitimate source of concern for the recipient states, but the level of transparency

---

4   Gilpin argues that the role of domestic economies and the differences among them determine the international economic affairs. Therefore, the differences among national systems of political economies have significant implications for the global economy. For more information see Robert Gilpin, *Global Political Economy of International Relations* (Princeton: Princeton University Press, 1987).

should not become the sole or primary basis on which policy makers assess the funds. The assumption that the level of transparency can serve as an indicator of the real agenda of a SWF is superficial, naïve, and most importantly, logically flawed.[5] A fully transparent SWF may include non–commercial principles in its investment decision making processes, as is the case with the Norwegian fund. A lack of transparency simply means that we do not know enough about these funds. This book attempts to fill this gap by providing a systematic typology of SWFs and an in–depth analysis of selected funds.

The study of SWFs at this junction in time is important as we are now on the verge of a new era of increased state intervention in the economy. On the one hand, states "have asserted their authority in global finance not as regulator but as major investors in the markets."[6] On the other hand—specifically after the recent crisis—they have taken over a number of large companies; as it is said:

> Today big government is back with a vengeance: not just as a brute fact, but as a vigorous ideology ... The world is seeing the rise of a new economic hybrid— what might be termed "state capitalism" ... The most interesting arguments over the next few years will weigh government failure against market failure.[7]

Interestingly, history is repeating itself. In the late 1960s, the expansion of multi–national companies (MNCs) raised concerns among both politicians and academics that the rise of the new global actors would undermine nation–states.[8] Today, policy makers' minds are occupied with the same fundamental concerns— the loss of sovereign power. The study of SWFs requires a "paradigm shift" in our approach to the study of international political economy.

This book provides information, analysis, and a research methodology that is of benefit to academia and policy makers alike. For the academic world, this research proposes a systematic methodology for a longitudinal study of SWFs. By drawing upon major international political economic theories, this book provides a much broader view of the functioning of SWFs. It emphasizes the need for more specific policies on both the international and domestic scales.

There are also several messages for policy makers at the national and international level. On the national level, they need to be more open to and receptive of emerging state capitalism. Policy makers can, in fact, influence the

---

5   For more information see Manda Shemirani, "Sovereign Wealth Funds: The False Promise of Transparency," *Infinity Journal* 1, no. 5 (2009).

6   Eric Helleiner, "The Geopolitics of Sovereign Wealth Funds: An Introduction," *Geopolitics* 14, no. 2 (2009).

7   "Leviathan Stirs Again; the Growth of the State," *The Economist*, 23 January 2010.

8   Scholars like Raymond Vernon (1971) and George Ball (1967) strongly believed that MNCs would undermine the states' sovereignty or would create conflict with state's goals.

flow of foreign portfolio investments, by, for instance, providing incentives that serve to direct the capital to areas that the recipient states prefer. Recipient states should also be conscious of the fact that vulnerabilities go both ways. Although less widely reported, investor states are concerned with the various political or financial risks to which their overseas investments are exposed. Recipient states can also learn from the investor states and create their own sovereign funds in order to entertain growing public expenditures, instead of simply passing the financial burden on to the tax payers.

On the international level, forums such as the International Working Group of SWFs (IWG) and later the International Forum of SWFs—both sponsored by the International Monetary Fund (IMF)—can foster greater transparency and cooperation among the investor states on the international level. The creation of the Generally Accepted Principles and Practices (GAPP), also known as the Santiago Principles, is only the first step in promoting good governance and greater transparency. Further efforts that directly engage both the investor and recipient states on an international level can provide further opportunity for knowledge transfer and conflict resolution.

The current book also addresses the popular question of whether SWFs pose a threat to the sovereignty or national security of recipient states. The question is best addressed by focusing on the more fundamental questions of why SWFs were created, what goals they pursue, and how the investor states balance various goals. An important consideration is that both investor states and their sovereign funds are prone to change over time. This is because both the international environment and the state's domestic structure (in all its political, economic, social, and cultural aspects) change over time. As a result, states' priorities shift as a response, and with that, so does the purpose of their sovereign funds. SWFs are live creatures that evolve over time and may pursue multiple goals. Therefore, a single theoretical perspective is not sufficient for the study of SWFs.

As mentioned earlier, despite the multiplicity of goals, there are certain conditions under which SWFs are expected to exhibit a similar behavior. We expect states to use the assets of their SWFs in times of economic hardship or when faced with global financial crises in order to cope with short–term financial problems. This means that during these times, SWFs would have to temporarily abandon their normal agenda and shift their focus to the more immediate goal of domestic economic stabilization, and in doing so, provide financial resources for various government rescue or stimulus packages. The study of selected SWFs during the recent global financial crisis showed that all of them provided, in various forms, resources for dealing with the crisis.

On the other hand, during times of normal economic activity (that is, when the states are not financially constrained), we would expect investor states to pursue their original goals for the SWFs. This book draws upon the major international political economic theories and proposes three alternatives to the mainstream economic argument of balance of payments smoothing. These alternative theoretical perspectives are subsequently applied to the selected SWFs.

Each political economic perspective looks at the state from a different angle. The first draws upon the most prominent theory in international relations, realism. The "economic statecraft" argument focuses on the classical concept of power in international relations theory and the notion that states pursue policies that maximize their power through various means. Having stakes in other states' economies or in certain industries can be a source of power for the investor states. SWFs, through their overseas investments, manage and accumulate national wealth and create interdependencies between the investor and recipient states. What can be hypothesized is that investor states use their SWFs in order to exert political power and influence over the recipient state.

The second theoretical perspective focuses solely on the state, in its role as an independent economic agent and entrepreneur. As states' assets have grown over time, so has the opportunity cost of holding these assets in the form of idle reserves. As mentioned earlier, global inflation and the exchange rate volatility have contributed to the increasing costs of holding idle reserves. As rational economic agents, states may seek alternative ways to better utilize available resources and maximize their wealth. In fact, this is not the first time that states have gotten directly involved in the economy.

State–owned enterprises (SOEs), many of which still exist today, are a prominent example of states' involvement in the economy. Similarly, investor states have attempted—much like private sector entrepreneurs—to take advantage of available opportunities (although not always successfully), and invest their funds in areas with the highest expected return consistent with their level of risk tolerance. The hypothesis is that investor states employ their SWFs for the sole purpose of efficient management of national wealth.

The third theoretical perspective uses the dynamics of the relationship between the state and the domestic structure on the one hand and the external forces of the global political economy on the other, to explain the state's management of sovereign funds. According to this view, investor states use SWFs in order to compensate the society for domestic deficiencies (economic, political or both). In fact, there are many arguments that speak to the necessity of domestic compensation, including embedded liberalism and a new compromise; the problem of smallness and domestic adjustments to external forces (in the case of small states); and the resource curse or the Dutch Disease argument (in the case of resource–abundant states). These three arguments, which overlap somewhat, can explain how SWFs use national financial assets to compensate domestic actors and how they provide resources for the redistribution of wealth among those who incur costs. Accordingly, we can hypothesize that SWFs are intended for domestic compensation purposes.

This book looks at world's four largest sovereign funds, including the most and the least transparent funds. The SWFs of Norway, United Arab Emirates, Singapore, and Russia provide an intriguing laboratory for the study of state capitalism. In conducting the current research, I have relied upon information and analyses provided by various institutions, market intelligence, press releases, and local and international media. The book will discuss the operation of the selected SWFs over a period of time, including times of economic prosperity and times of hardship. Subsequently, I will compare the funds' behavior during the two periods to determine various goals pursued by the SWFs.

Chapter 2 briefly reviews the alternative perspectives that can explain the creation and functioning of SWFs. This chapter discusses the merits and applicability of economic statecraft, state entrepreneurship, and domestic compensation perspectives. The chapter also presents a systematic typology and comparisons of the world's twenty–largest SWFs, based on various criteria including, scale, source of funding, transparency, and perceived objectives. Of these criteria, two have been the most critical: transparency and objectives. Based on these two criteria, four major case studies are the selected: the Government Pension Fund–Global of Norway, the Abu Dhabi Investment Authority of the United Arab Emirates, Temasek of Singapore, and the National Wealth Fund of Russia. The chapter introduces a set of qualifying questions (or markers) in order to test the hypotheses mentioned earlier.

The case studies section starts with the study of the fund of Norway, a highly transparent fund that will set the level of expectations high with respect to the volume of data required for the analysis. Chapter 3 examines the Government Pension Fund–Global—one of the world's largest SWFs, with total assets under management of approximately $441 billion (2,763 Krone[9]) as of end of the first quarter of 2010. The creation of the fund and its role during periods of large budget deficits—specifically during the latest global financial crisis—has been consistent with both the economic and domestic compensation perspectives. In the absence of financial constraints, the fund has pursued a defined risk–return margin through a portfolio focused on equities. The fund's commercial performance, however, has been constrained by a set of non–economic guidelines that are expressions of the national political consensus in Norway. The fund, in fact, pursues multiple goals including profitability and socially–responsible investment, in accordance to the state's foreign policy agenda, as encapsulated in the Ethical Guidelines. The pursuit of foreign policy through the fund, however, was limited to unilateral and relatively small–scale sanctions through negative screening of or divestment from various states or companies.

Chapter 4 looks at the Abu Dhabi Investment Authority (ADIA), another of the world's largest funds, with an estimated value of between $400 billion and $875 billion[10] as estimated prior to the recent global financial crisis. This fund remains one of the least transparent funds. Notwithstanding the Emirate's claims of rapid modernization, many domestic political and administrative processes—including the management of the fund—still reflect an adherence to traditional

---

9   "Government Pension Fund-Global, First Quarter 2010," (Oslo: Norges Bank Investment Management 2010).

10   Andrew England, "ADIA Makes Play for a Native Minority," *Financial Times*, 16 November 2008.

values. Evidence suggests that the fund's operation is more consistent with state entrepreneurship and domestic compensation perspectives than economic statecraft or balance of payments correction theses. The emphasis on equities in the portfolio shows that achieving high returns is a more significant goal. Both the emirate of Abu Dhabi and the United Arab Emirates have little domestic tax base and remain heavily dependent on the petroleum sector. Abu Dhabi, as the richest emirate, has also provided financial support to the federal budget and other emirates on various occasions.[11] Although there is no information as to whether the Abu Dhabi fund provided the bailout funds, it is nevertheless important to recognize, on a broader scale, the need for financial resources for domestic compensation.

In Chapter 5, I will examine Temasek of Singapore. Temasek is an interesting case because unlike the majority of SWFs, which are funded by proceeds from the resource sector, it was initially endowed with a portfolio of state–owned companies. Therefore, the fund's portfolio consists for the most part of equities from the beginning. Another unique feature of this fund is the issue of corporate bonds for the financing of its operations. State involvement in the economy is undeniable; however, the entrepreneurial spirit has become embedded in the management of various state–owned companies. Temasek has acted mainly as the entrepreneurial arm of the government and has facilitated the process of privatization by managing the state's equities in various business areas. The fund's structure and management follow corporate models and are relatively transparent. Temasek has established a sophisticated network of subsidiaries and is active both locally and internationally. There is no evidence indicating that the fund has ever been used either as a precautionary instrument for coping with external financial shocks, or as a foreign policy tool, mainly because withdrawals from national reserves (including those held by Temasek) are legally or constitutionally prohibited.

The last case study is examined in Chapter 6. The National Wealth Fund of Russia provides a unique opportunity for the study of a fund in its nascent stage. The idea of establishing a precautionary (stabilization) fund was formed against the background of the difficult times following the collapse of the communist system. Of the three political economy perspectives under consideration, the domestic compensation thesis is the most relevant to the Russian fund today. The fund has been the focus of various centers of power within the Russian government. But the constant domestic struggle over access to the fund's assets has resulted in the fund's inability to develop a solid agenda. There was no evidence showing that the state has acted as an entrepreneur in managing the fund's assets, mainly due to lack of entrepreneurial talent and spirit—something that is often times confused with rent–seeking behavior. Moreover, the fund's assets were mostly held in cash or lent to domestic banks or businesses, in the wake of the recent financial crisis and as a part of the government stimulus package. The Russian fund certainly has

---

11   In fact Abu Dhabi provided billions of dollars for the purpose of bailing out various troubled projects in Dubai, the most prominent one being the world's tallest building (Burj Khalifa, formerly known as Burj Dubai).

a long way to go in the development of a solid agenda, investment framework, and independent and strong management—if indeed it ever manages achieving those goals. Conditions are bound to change; nevertheless, the fund presents a unique opportunity to observe the dynamics and challenges of institution–building within a state that has undergone a relatively recent and major transition.

A summary of all the findings and a comparative analysis of all four SWFs are presented in Chapter 7. As mentioned earlier, the dynamic nature of investor states and their SWFs, as well as the multiplicity of goals, has made application of a single theoretical perspective inadequate. This book proposes a systematic methodology for the study of these funds over their life span and emphasizes the need for a paradigm shift in our approach towards the study of state capitalism.

References

Cohen, Benjamin J. "Sovereign Wealth Funds and National Security: The Great Tradeoff." *International Affairs* 85, no. 4 (2009): 713-31.

England, Andrew. "ADIA Makes Play for a Native Minority." *Financial Times*, 16 November 2008.

Gilpin, Robert. *Global Political Economy of International Relations*. Princeton: Princeton University Press, 1987.

"Government Pension Fund-Global, First Quarter 2010." Oslo: Norges Bank Investment Management 2010.

Helleiner, Eric. "The Geopolitics of Sovereign Wealth Funds: An Introduction." *Geopolitics* 14, no. 2 (2009): 300-04.

Hufbauer, Gary Clyde, Yee Wong, and Ketki Sheth. *US–China Trade Disputes: Rising Tide, Rising Stakes*, Policy Analyses in International Economics 78: Peterson Institute for International Economics, 2006.

"Leviathan Stirs Again; the Growth of the State." *The Economist*, 23 January 2010, 23-26.

Shemirani, Manda. "Sovereign Wealth Funds: The False Promise of Transparency." *Infinity Journal* 1, no. 5 (2009).

"Sovereign Wealth Funds–a Work Agenda." International Monetary Fund, 2008.

Chapter 2
We Know More Than We Think

One of the main questions that the current research attempts to answer is what the purposes of sovereign funds are, in other words, what goals investor states are pursuing. While many have wondered as to how to address questions like these, the rich literature of international political economy readily provides several explanations for the behavior of investor states. Before we proceed with answering the question, we first need to define exactly what we mean by SWFs and where they come from. Afterwards, we will take a look at some of SWFs and compare their size on both global and domestic scales. An overview and comparison based on two important characteristics of major SWFs, i.e., level of transparency and perceived objectives, will provide us with a basis for the final choice of case studies. A review of the political economic theories will also help us in outlining the critical questions that could be used in determining the underlying motives and goals of the SWFs.

You Can Measure Only What You Can Define

In fact, there is no universally accepted definition for SWFs. The year 2007 saw efforts by many policymakers and researchers to define the emerging phenomenon of SWFs. In June, the US Treasury stated: "The term 'SWF' means a government investment vehicle which is funded by foreign exchange assets, and which manages those assets separately from the official reserves at central banks." Later in November, Edwin Truman from the Peterson Institute for International Economics, a Washington–based think tank and a former Director of the Division of International Finance at the Federal Reserve Board, introduced SWFs to the United States House Committee on Banking, Housing, and Urban Affairs as "separate pools of international assets owned and managed by governments to achieve a variety of economic and financial objectives."[1]

OECD defines SWFs as "government–owned investment vehicles that are funded by foreign exchange assets." Morgan Stanley assigns five characteristics to SWFs: being sovereign, and having high foreign currency exposure, no explicit

---

1   The United States Senate Committee on Banking, Housing and Urban Affairs, *Testimony of Edwin M. Truman, Senior Fellow, Peterson Institute for International Economics*, 14 November 2007.

liabilities, high risk tolerance, and a long–term investment horizon.[2] All through this book, SWFs are considered as "funds that are owned by the sovereign states governments or major sub–national governments, that have no monetary or financial regulatory function, and whose investment criteria include provisions for overseas investment."

This definition includes, for instance, Abu Dhabi Investment Authority (ADIA), a sub–national fund of United Arab Emirates with one of the world's largest assets and overseas investments, as well as Government Pension Fund–Global of Norway, but excludes Saudi Arabia Monetary Authority (SAMA), which sets the country's overall monetary policy and regulates commercial banks, and exchange dealers.

Origins of SWFs

The first group of SWFs was established in the early 1950s, some in 1970s, but the majority of sovereign funds were created after the mid–1990s. Many argue that the creation of SWFs was a result of rapid accumulation of foreign reserves. In fact the global reserves have been increasing steadily since the 1990s. Between 2001 and 2007, global reserves almost tripled from $2.1 trillion to $6.2 trillion, with the developing countries accounting for more than 80 percent of those reserves.[3] Current account surplus was the main drive behind the accumulation of reserves. This is especially the case of commodity or oil exporting countries, e.g., China, Singapore, Venezuela and the Middle Eastern states. For a few other countries, the capital account played a more important role in building up the reserves. For instance, India, Mexico, and Colombia sought large external financing.[4]

Some analysts have attributed the creation of sovereign funds to the accumulation of international reserves "in excess of what may be needed for intervention or balance–of–payment purposes."[5] Some others have viewed this phenomenon in terms of widening of global current account imbalances due to shifts in global savings and investment patterns, and, more specifically, the rapid growth of the foreign exchange reserves of non–Western countries:

> As foreign exchange reserves have grown, many monetary authorities have concluded that these reserves are well in excess of their immediate needs and offer sufficient protection against sudden capital outflows. Thus, they have opted

2   "Sovereign Wealth Funds–a Work Agenda," (International Monetary Fund, 2008), 37-38.

3   Stephany Griffith-Jones and José Antonio Ocampo, *Sovereign Wealth Funds: A Developing Country Perspective*, Workshop on Sovereign Wealth Funds (London: Andean Development Corporation 2008).

4   Ibid.

5   Roland Beck and Michael Fidora, "The Impact of Sovereign Wealth Funds on Global Financial Markets," (European Central Bank, 2008), 6.

to "ring–fence" a portion of their foreign exchange reserves for other purposes, allocating a significant share to sovereign wealth funds.[6]

In the case of the SWFs of developing countries, some scholars believe that:

> The growth of these funds are part of larger process of accumulation of foreign exchange assets by developing countries, which also includes the large accumulation of foreign exchange reserves during the boom that these countries have experienced over most of the current decades, reflecting both booming exports (due in part to high commodity, particularly mineral prices) and pro–cyclical capital flows.[7]

Interestingly, the majority of states that have established sovereign funds are resource–abundant, with the main resources being oil and gas. Therefore, many have concluded that there must be a direct connection between the creation of SWFs and the price of oil.[8] The idea is intuitive and straightforward: an increase in oil prices means an increase in the value of the country's main export (oil), and a subsequent windfall of foreign currency (US dollars). At the McKinsey Global Institute, creation of sovereign funds is explained within this context of high oil prices and the windfall of petro–dollars: "[m]ost oil–exporting countries have set up state–owned investment funds, often called sovereign wealth funds, to invest oil surpluses in global financial assets."[9]

Recent booms in international commodity prices have also enabled other commodity–exporting countries like Chile (copper), Kiribati (phosphate), and Botswana (diamonds and minerals) to accumulate foreign exchange as a result of the build–up in their balance of payments. There are also a number of non–commodity exporting countries across Southeast Asia and Oceania, including Singapore, Indonesia, China, South Korea, Malaysia, Hong Kong, Australia, and New Zealand that have managed to accumulate foreign reserves over time. These countries share a number of characteristics, including an abundant labor force coupled with wages lower than those of the western countries, as well as established merchant marine facilities. These countries have also been major hubs for international trade, specifically, assembly and production of high–tech goods that are exported back to the industrial world. Many of these Southeast Asian countries have managed to accumulate foreign reserves over time.

---

6   Shams Butt et al., "Sovereign Wealth Funds: A Growing Global Force in Corporate Finance," *Journal of Applied Corporate Finance* 20, no. 1 (2008): 74.

7   Griffith-Jones and Ocampo, *Sovereign Wealth Funds: A Developing Country Perspective*, 2.

8   The only exception is Venezuela that created Macroeconomic Stabilization Fund in 1998, following the IMF advice. For most of the 1980s, world oil prices have been declining from year to year.

9   Diana Farrell and Susan Lund, "The New Role of Oil Wealth in the World Economy," *McKinsey Quarterly* January(2008).

There is no doubt that the availability of resources (in this case foreign reserves or balance of payments surplus) determines a state's ability to create a sovereign fund in the first place. For many resource–exporting countries, the state's international financial status has been directly dependent on the global price of their main export. According to the economic view, the main purpose of the SWFs is to provide financial stabilization or smoothing effect on the domestic economy. Edwin Truman from the Peterson Institute for International Economics refers to this objective as *fiscal treatment*, saying: "Fiscal Treatment is central to a SWF's role in the macro–economic stability of the country."[10] From the economic standpoint, sovereign funds are saving or stabilization funds, i.e., a vehicle for the store of national wealth and protection against unfavorable changes in international reserves.

In other words, sovereign funds can absorb the impact of external economic shocks or neutralize pressures on exchange rates due to the inflow of foreign exchange. These shocks are usually related to pro–cyclical changes in both the price and volume of exports:

> SWFs—especially stabilization funds—can help shield an economy against volatility in markets of critical value for an economy, such as oil or other commodities. In this case, the fund serves as a liquidity pool which is replenished at times of favorable commodity price conditions or reserve inflows, and which can be drawn upon in cases of low asset prices or shortage of reserves.[11]

SWFs can absorb excess liquidity or foreign exchange at times of high export revenues. These reserves can be redistributed back to the economy when there is a shortage of foreign exchange. These funds can also be used to neutralize the impact of unexpected changes in national consumption longitudinally, although little explanation is offered with respect to the redistribution mechanism. SWFs can "smooth the country's inter–temporal consumption, in ways similar to individuals who save both for their retirement and to leave an inheritance to their children."[12]

Other terms used to describe the purpose of SWFs include store of wealth in the case of resource–exporting countries, fiscal stabilization, and self–insurance against pro–cyclical capital inflow (e.g., Griffith–Jones and Ocampo 2008), foreign exchange sterilization and stand alone investment in excess of the "optimal" reserve levels (e.g., Kimmitt 2008). Almost all of these goals are just reiteration of the same ideas, i.e., income (or consumption) smoothing and protection against fiscal or foreign exchange volatility.

---

10   Edwin M. Truman, "A Scoreboard for Sovereign Wealth Funds," in *Conference on China's Exchange Rate Policy* (Washington D.C.: Peterson Institute for International Economics, 2007), 3.

11   Steffen Kern, "Sovereign Wealth Funds–State Investments on the Rise," (Deutsche Bank, 2007), 4.

12   Griffith-Jones and Ocampo, *Sovereign Wealth Funds: A Developing Country Perspective*, 9.

SWFs: a Reality Check

Today, states that own a SWF range from advanced large economies to resource–
dependant small countries. Additionally, SWFs differ in their size, source of
funding, investment approach, level of transparency, and perceived objectives.
One of the main attributes of a SWF is its scale. One can assess the size of these
funds in several ways. The simplest would be to evaluate the volume of each fund
in absolute terms. However, the absolute values would not tell us anything about
the significance of these funds on global scale, or compared to the size of the
owner state's economy.

A meaningful way of capturing the scale of a fund is to look at its size relative
to the size of the source economy. Alternatively, we can express the size of the
fund relative to the total market capitalization of a major stock exchange such as
New York Stock Exchange (NYSE) or London Stock Exchange (LSE). Table 2.1
presents a comparison of several funds based on various scales.[13] Depending on
our measure a fund may be among the largest on the domestic scale, but very small
on the global scale, and vice versa. For instance, the fund of Brunei is the second
largest on the domestic scale. However, on a global scale this fund amounts to only
about 0.8 percent of the LSE or 0.2 percent of the NYSE market capitalization.

Table 2.1   A Comparison between various SWF

	Estimated Asset Value ($ billion)	As a percentage of GDP	As a percentage of LSE	As a percentage of NYSE
Abu Dhabi Investment Authority, UAE	627.0	521	23.1	5.7
Brunei Investment Agency	30.0	309	1.1	0.3
Kuwait Investment Authority	202.8	269	5.6	1.4
Government Investment Corporation, Singapore	247.5	169	5.7	1.4
Qatar Investment Authority	65.0	158	2.4	0.6
Government Pension Fund – Global, Norway	443.0	103	10.0	2.5
China Investment Corporation	288.8	0.03	5.3	1.3

Source: Lyons, "State Capitalism: The Rise of Sovereign Wealth Funds" and "Sovereign
Wealth Fund Institute." http://swfinstitute.org/.

---

13   The ratios are based on pre–financial crisis figures of 2006 GDP, LSE, and NYSE
market capitalization.

In addition to their size, SWFs differ in their sources of funding. The majority of the funds are financed directly through the proceeds from the commodity exports, with the main commodity typically being petroleum and gas. These countries include, for instance, Kuwait, United Arab Emirates, Norway, Russia, Brunei, Algeria, and Azerbaijan. Chile is one of few non–petroleum commodity exporting states, with its Pension Reserve and Social and Economic Stabilization Fund financed through the export of copper. For non–commodity based fund, the financing typically comes through the foreign exchange reserves already held by various official organizations such as the central bank or the ministry of economy or finance. In the case of Malaysia and Taiwan, the funds are partially financed through debt and in case of Temasek of Singapore, in the form share holdings of government–owned companies.

Perhaps one of the most important characteristics of SWFs, one that has created a row of criticism and controversy, is the level of transparency. Assessing transparency can be very subjective. For example, Standard Chartered Bank and Oxford Analytica, in a joint report on SWFs, categorized the world's twenty largest funds as either "very low," "low," "medium," or "high."[14] According to their measure, funds that "provide detailed information on their size, returns achieved and their portfolio composition"—such as, that of Norway, Singapore, Malaysia, Canada, and Azerbaijan—are categorized as highly transparent.[15] However, they provide no further details regarding the basis on which the other funds are categorized.

Carl Linaburg and Michael Maduell from the SWF Institute created the Linaburg–Maduell (L–M) Transparency Index that rates the SWFs on a one–to–ten scale based on funds characteristics such as availability of independently audited annual reports, information on ownership structure and management, financial data (portfolio structure and return), and finally fund's contact information and website. The critical issue is that the concept of transparency is susceptible to change. Therefore the transparency ratings can change as funds release additional information, voluntarily or under pressure from international organizations. For instance, Temasek Holdings of Singapore initially received an eight on L–M scale in 2008 and early 2009, but was upgraded to ten (fully transparent) in late 2009.[16] As of June 2010, the most transparent funds included those of Norway, Singapore, Chile, Canada, Australia, and South Korea, while the funds of United Arab Emirates, Russia, China, Oman, and Brunei are among the most opaque funds, according to the SWF Institute.

Lack of transparency not only limits our understanding of the functioning and objectives of the funds, but also makes us believe that opaque funds are deliberately hiding information as well. Obviously, SWFs were created to serve

---

14   Gerard Lyons, "State Capitalism: The Rise of Sovereign Wealth Funds," (Standard Chartered Bank, 2007).

15   Ibid., 7.

16   "Sovereign Wealth Fund Institute," http://swfinstitute.org/.

various purposes. Some of these funds, like that of Russia, were initially created as stabilization funds with the primary objective of insulating and protecting the domestic economy against fluctuations in global commodity prices, or as a backup in the event of sanctions. A small number of SWFs were established as pension funds (or pension reserves). These funds, presumably, act as long–term reserves for meeting future national pension obligations. Loss of income due to the depletion of non–renewable energy resources was the reason that a number of other states, like Norway, established a fund for future generations. The socio–economic development and the restructuring and promotion of domestic industries are the reasons behind the inception of other funds.

All these objectives are, more or less, precautionary in nature and the funds may pursue one or more of them at any given time. There are, on the other hand, a number of other states—including the United Arab Emirates, China, and Singapore—that may be concerned about the opportunity cost of holding idle assets and therefore seek to achieve high returns. One would expect such funds to have a portfolio which is focused more on riskier assets.

Generally, we can categorize precautionary funds as those with the immediate objects of protecting the domestic economy against international market fluctuations, supporting economic sectors or industries, or meeting future national obligations such as public pensions. On the other hand, we can categorize funds with a higher risk tolerance and immediate objective of maximizing return on assets as speculative funds.

Two of the above criteria, i.e., the degree of transparency and objectives, have been the source of much debate among politicians and academics recently. Figure 2.1 combines these two important characteristics for the selected funds with total asset value of over $100 billion. The funds with an L–M Transparency Index of six and above are considered "transparent" and the rest "opaque."[17] With respect to the objectives, those funds with the goal (whether explicitly stated or not) of either saving for the future—including meeting future public pension obligations, preserving the value of non–renewable energy resources for future generations, or long–term developmental goals—or for balance of payments stabilization are considered "precautionary." Funds with no clear agenda or those with an immediate focus on the current value of the fund and the maximization of its returns—including those with investment diversification strategies, return maximization agenda, or greater emphasis on equity markets—are considered "speculative."

The final selection of SWFs as case studies in this book is derived from Figure 2.1. The selected cases represent the most significant (sizable) fund in each

---

17   The L–M index rates the SWFs on a one–to–ten scale according to the essential principles of transparency presented by Linaburg and Maduell. Although this index provides a good starting point for measuring transparency, some of the criteria—e.g., availability of address and phone number of the fund and the maintenance of the fund's webpage—are too simplistic.

quadrant. The size of the fund matters, particularly when it is compared with other funds or assessed in connection with the market capitalization of a major stock exchange like the NYSE or LSE. The assumption is that, the larger the fund, the greater its potential impact on global financial markets, and, in turn, its importance in global studies. Taking the above considerations into account, the final selection includes SWFs of Norway, United Arab Emirates (ADIA), Singapore (Temasek), and Russia.

It should be mentioned that the current approach focuses on the characteristics of the SWFs and then analyses their performance within a larger context of the political economy. Another approach in the study of SWFs is a top–down approach whereby based on the characteristics of the owner state (type of the government or the economic system) and the performance of the SWF is explained. Since the purpose of the book is to investigate the creation and functioning of SWFs, the primary focus has been on individual funds hence the above case selection methodology.

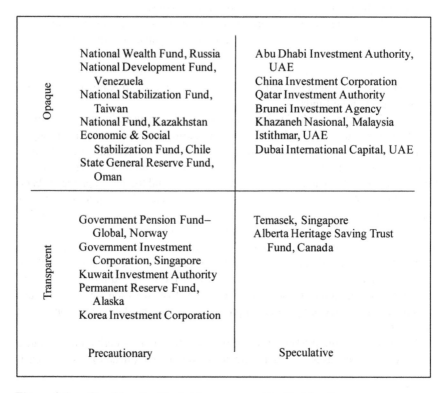

Figure 2.1   Combined criteria: transparency and objectives

Sources: Lyons, "State Capitalism: The Rise of Sovereign Wealth Funds" and "Sovereign Wealth Fund Institute." http://swfinstitute.org/.

The Government Pension Fund–Global (GPF–Global) of Norway is one of the most transparent funds, with a precautionary agenda, as well as a clear investment strategy. This fund is owned and managed by a well–established European democracy with an inherently open economy. The Norwegian case can be used as a benchmark for assessing other funds in a number of areas, including performance, governance, and transparency. The GPF–Global has the largest assets in its class of transparent–precautionary funds. It can also serve as a good example for other funds and for current and future efforts in formulating codes of conduct and global governance.

In the class of transparent–speculative funds, I have chosen Temasek of Singapore, which also is representative of East Asian economies. Although categorized as transparent, its L–M Transparency Index was below that of the Norwegian fund. In terms of assets, Temasek is much larger than Alberta Heritage Fund, the other fund in this class. In terms of characteristics, Temasek is a unique fund because it was endowed—instead of cash—with the government holdings in various public companies. The Abu Dhabi Investment Authority (ADIA) of the United Arab Emirates is another interesting case. This fund manages one of the world's largest pools of assets, both in absolute and relative terms. At the same time, it is one of the low–transparency funds. This fund has already acquired stakes in financial institutions and other industries both in the region and in Europe.

Russia has the largest fund in the class of non–transparent and precautionary funds. The Russian fund also adds another dimension—and perhaps a complication—to the case selection, i.e., while the other selected sovereign funds are a few decades old, the Russian fund—which was established in 2004—represents a class of emerging SWFs. Only recently, in February 2008, the Stabilization Fund of Russia was split into two funds, one managing official reserves, while the other—which is referred to as "National Wealth Fund"—became the official Sovereign Wealth Fund. Although the Russian fund does not have much overseas investments at the moment, partial ownership of, or even expressions of interest in the infrastructure sectors of other countries (such as Germany) have raised concerns.

Having decided on the SWFs cases, we now need to have a clear roadmap for the study of these funds. That means we first have to identify critical questions, in order to be able to determine why SWFs were created, what goals they pursue, and how the investor states balance various goals. As briefly discussed earlier, theoretical perspectives, especially those in the field of international political economy, can enhance our understanding of the purpose and functioning of SWFs. These perspectives will in fact define our ultimate critical questions.

The orthodox economic view contends that SWFs are the product of foreign reserve surpluses, due to high commodity prices or, in case of oil–exporting countries, a windfall of petrodollars. The economists generally explain the purpose of such funds in terms of balance of payments corrections, neutralizing external economic shocks, or inter–temporal wealth smoothing. By viewing the creation of SWFs solely in terms of absorbing economic shocks or smoothing inter–generational income and consumption, however, economists close the door to other possible motives (political or social) that had led the states to establish such funds. For instance, we do not know why SWFs, unlike other types of national reserves, have entered equity and real–estate markets with higher risk than virtually risk–free bonds such as the US treasury bills. Moreover, why SWFs develop multiple goals and how they balance these goals against each other are further questions where the economic argument falls short. _

In fact, economics is only one side of the story. States may have decided to establish sovereign funds for reasons other than economic smoothing or shock absorbing. Moreover, the economic view does not adequately explain the cases where funds may have expanded or maintained the status quo at times of economic contraction, or actively managed during the time of plenty. The economic view also does not shed light on the internal politics as well as the dynamics of decision making and policy setting within the funds, or the nature of the relationship between the fund management and the state leadership.

Sovereign wealth funds are technically a part of the state's political apparatus and can be used for reasons related to the domestic political and socioeconomic structure of the country. At the same time, these funds are significant financial actors. The theoretical literature in international political economy can provide valuable alternative explanations for SWFs' motives, as well as the multiplicity of goals and the dynamics of investment decision making within these funds. These views combine economics with political science and while they may not be mutually exclusive, they can enhance our understanding of the operation and evolution of sovereign funds.

The political economic literature also speaks to the issue of the evolution and transformation of sovereign funds' objectives over time. Interestingly, each of the political economic perspectives looks at the state from a different angle. One draws upon the most prominent theory in international relations, i.e., realism, while another focuses solely on the state in its role as an independent economic agent and an entrepreneur. Other perspectives look at the dynamics of the relationship between the state and the domestic structure on the one hand and the external forces of the global political economy on the other hand to explain the state's management of sovereign funds. Before introducing the ultimate questions, a brief review of the political economic perspective is essential.

What Political Economy Tells Us About SWFs

There are three mainstream political economic perspectives that can be applied to the study of SWFs and help explaining why there are differences among SWFs with respect to their objectives as well as level of transparency. The first view starts with the classical concept of power in international relations theory and draws upon the notion of power put forward by contemporary political scientists. States pursue policies that maximize their power in all areas, including economics and commerce. The second perspective views states as capitalist economic agents or, more precisely, as entrepreneurs. Although states' assets may have grown over time, so has the opportunity cost of holding idle reserves, especially in the light of global inflation and the downward pressure on US dollar. As capitalist entrepreneurs, investor states have attempted to take advantage of the existing opportunities and invest their money in areas that they expect to yield higher returns. Finally, the third theoretical view ties the state's management of national assets to the domestic structure of the country, arguing that sovereign funds are a means of compensating society for structural deficiencies (economic, political or both). This perspective can explain how SWFs manage national financial assets for domestic compensation and how they provide resources for redistribution of wealth among those who incur costs and whose consensus is critical to the continuity of the political regime.

Realism and Economic Statecraft

Much of the recent debate on SWFs has derived from one of the most prominent perspectives in international relations theory, i.e., realism, with its focus on the concept of power. Political elites, especially in the United States, have been overwhelmingly concerned with the realist view and the potential for manipulation of economic and financial power by states that have employed SWFs to acquire stakes in various economic sectors overseas.

At the core of realism lies the notion of power, its sources and forms. A strain of realists including Thucydides and the mercantilists draw a close linkage between power and security concerns on the one hand and economic affairs on the other hand. Thucydides considered wealth to be an important source of military power, as he wrote: "war is a matter not so much of arms as of money, which makes arms of use."[18] Mercantilists believed that a state's power depended on the amount of gold and silver it could accumulate in the public treasury. This wealth would enable the state to build up its military.

Although physical resources and capabilities—including the stock of arms, wealth, population and land—have traditionally been the main underpinning of national strength, the contemporary idea of power goes far beyond the resources and capabilities. In the 1970s and 1980s, scholars began to return to a "realist conception of the relationship of economics and politics that had disappeared from postwar American writings."[19] The postwar instability of economic systems due to global changes—including the emergence of new transnational actors like the Organization of Petroleum Exporting Countries (OPEC), increased competition between the United States, Japan and Europe, the relative decline of the American

---

18   Thucydides, *The History of the Peloponnesian War* (New York: Dutton, 1910), 41.

19   Robert Gilpin, *Global Political Economy of International Relations* (Princeton: Princeton University Press, 1987), xii.

hegemony, and the debt crises of Southeast Asian countries—forced realists to "confront the fact that economic issues were of central importance and could no longer be relegated to the category of 'low politics'."[20]

Susan Strange identified the structure of production as one of the facets of power and defined it as "the sum of all arrangements determining what is produced, by whom and for whom, by what method and on what terms."[21] She argued that the production structure is what creates wealth in a political economy, which is also a source of power. She also asserted that there is a connection between the locus of power in the society and the production structure, and that when the structure of production changes, significant changes may follow in the distribution of social and political power. But perhaps the high point of Strange's argument is where she maintains:

> In the international political economy, power is held by those who can offer or deny security, and by those who manage creation of wealth ... The power to create credit implies the power to allow or to deny other people the possibility of spending today and paying back tomorrow, the power to let them exercise purchasing power and thus influence markets for production, and also the power to manage and mismanage the currency in which credit is denominated, thus affecting rates of exchange with credit denominated in other currencies.[22]

The study of economic statecraft has a long but still relevant tradition. Economic statecraft was in fact a critical component of United States foreign policy and grand strategy with respect to the containment of the Soviet Union during the Cold War. The scholarly literature on economic engagement as an instrument of statecraft has no better starting point than Hirschman's 1945 work, *National Power and the Structure of Foreign Trade*. Hirschman developed a systematic framework for analysis of the relationship between trade and political power and highlighted the importance of unequal trade relationships. Although Hirschman did not view the pursuit of power a necessary outcome of unbalanced economic relations, he argued that there is always a possibility that a government will use an unequal relationship as a source of power.[23]

For Baldwin, economic statecraft is the use of economic instruments by a government to influence the behavior of another state. He argued that economic statecraft can serve as a means of communicating intentions to friends and foes alike. Economic statecraft operates on multiple levels and is often an effective

20   Theodore H. Cohn, *Global Political Economy : Theory and Practice*, 2nd ed. (New York: Longman, 2003), 76.

21   Susan Strange, *States and Markets* (New York: Basil Blackwell, 1988), 62.

22   Ibid., 88.

23   Albert O. Hirschman, *National Power and the Structure of Foreign Trade* (Berkeley and Los Angeles: University of California Press, 1945).

means of achieving foreign policy goals.[24] This definition of economic statecraft has been mainly used in connection with economic sanctions or incentives, but in the context of contemporary global political economy it may be extended to SWFs as well. In fact, SWFs can serve as both a foreign policy tool and a precautionary reserve in the face of potential sanctions.

Additionally, in a world of highly interdependent financial markets, a state's power can extend well beyond its geographical borders. For instance, Haskel argues that in a world of highly interdependent political economies, an estimate of a state's power depends not only on the resources under its control but on the access that others have to its resources.[25] SWFs, by their very nature, create such interdependencies and access to other states' resources. From the recipient states' point of view, giving up significant stakes in industries or economic sectors to other states would mean relinquishing a part of their power to a foreign power.

SWFs also give rise to a variation in one of the prominent debates in international relations today, i.e., the security dilemma. States that create funds may do so for precautionary purposes, including protection against international market volatility and provisions in the event of sanctions. However, their choice of defensive tools (e.g., overseas investment) can be perceived by other states (mainly the recipients of sovereign investment) as a method of creating interdependencies that could be used for the exercise of political power.[26]

As mentioned earlier, a number of states that are recipients of SWFs' investment, mainly the United States, have expressed concern about the intention of such funds. These recipient states argue that the SWFs might have a hidden agenda, and that by acquiring significant stakes in different industries and economic sectors, they expose the recipient state to national security risks. If this is true, then we would expect the sovereign funds to have high risk tolerance with respect to market forces, acquire stakes in politically sensitive industries, and to continue to acquire stakes in such sectors even during market downturns.

State's Capitalist Entrepreneurship

Schumpeter's classic description of entrepreneurship as "a fundamental impulse that sets and keeps the capitalist engine in motion"[27] provides an appropriate

---

24   David A. Baldwin, *Economic Statecraft* (Princeton, N.J.: Princeton University Press, 1985).

25   Barbara Haskel, "Access to Society: A Neglected Dimension of Power," *International Organization* 34, no. 1 (1980).

26   There is a vast literature on offensive or defensive realism. Theoretical discussion on these two strains of realism is outside the scope of the current research. Suffice to say that despite changes in time and sources of power, the fundamental issue of security dilemma (here more of an economic or financial nature) still remains the same.

27   Joseph Schumpeter, *Capitalism, Socialism and Democracy* (New York: Harper and Row, 1962), 83.

starting point for the study of states as entrepreneurs. A number of states have recently been found to act as international investors, driven by risk and profit calculations. Sovereign fund investment can be viewed as a modern form of state entrepreneurship, for the purpose of extracting profit from global opportunities.

Kirzner argues that the entire role of an entrepreneur lies in its alertness to unnoticed opportunities and in the ability to subsequently exploit those opportunities. In other words, entrepreneurship not only involves identification of opportunities but also extracting profit from those opportunities. Moreover, entrepreneurship involves planning, learning, and innovation.[28] In fact, state entrepreneurship entails the same concepts (identification, learning, and innovation) and goals (profit maximization and risk management) as private sector entrepreneurship. There are a number of authors—both economists and political scientists—that have highlighted the role of states as entrepreneurs. Eisinger, for instance, refers to America as an entrepreneurial state that "performs roles much like those of Schumpeter's figure ... The difference between Schumpeter's entrepreneur and the entrepreneurial state is that the latter seeks to identify market opportunities not for its own exclusive gain but on behalf of private actors whose pursuit of those opportunities may serve public ends."[29]

Yu applied the very same concept of entrepreneurship to four Southeast Asian newly industrializing economies (NIEs), and showed that "governments can act as entrepreneurs and, through learning and innovation, can alter the given resource situation."[30] He further distinguished between "directive entrepreneurial intervention" (as in the cases of South Korea, Taiwan, and Singapore) and "facilitative entrepreneurial intervention" (as in the case of Hong Kong), and argued that with the active entrepreneurial intervention of governments, these NIEs became what the World Bank has referred to as the East Asian "miracle."[31] Other

---

28   Israel M. Kirzner, *Competition and Entrepreneurship* (Chicago: University of Chicago Press, 1973); ———, *Perception, Opportunity, and Profit: Studies in the Theory of Entrepreneurship* (Chicago: University of Chicago Press, 1979); ———, *Discovery and the Capitalist Process* (Chicago: University of Chicago Press, 1985).

29   Peter K. Eisinger, *The Rise of the Entrepreneurial State: State and Local Economic Development Policy in the United States*, La Follette Public Policy Series (Madison, Wis.: University of Wisconsin Press, 1988), 9.

30   Tony F. Yu, "Entrepreneurial State: The Role of Government in the Economic Development of the Asian Newly Industrialising Economies," *Development Policy Review* 15(1997): 60.

31   The terms "facilitative" and "directive" government intervention was used by Luedde–Neurath (1983). The first refers to function of government as the provider of public goods and the latter refers to achieving set of goals through conscious interference in markets and selective application of incentives and/or controls. Yu 1997 adopted the term and combined it with the idea of state entrepreneurship. For more information see: Richard Luedde-Neurath, "State Intervention and Export–Oriented Development in South Korea," in *Developmental States in East Asia*, ed. Gordon White (New York: St. Martin's Press, 1988), 103.

political scientists like Wade support this view and believe that the governments of East Asian countries intervened in the economy extensively, in the capacity of an entrepreneur, and promoted the development of industries, some of which became highly competitive internationally.[32]

The concept of state entrepreneurship is also embodied in the creation of state–owned enterprises (SOEs). Where markets failed, governments stepped in as economic agents. Toninelli argues that the creation of SOEs and the "increased role of the state in the economy as the manager–entrepreneur of scarce resources is a phenomenon with deep roots in the modern age."[33] He identified, among other things, social goals (including full employment) and market failure as reasons for the creation of public enterprises.

In a sense, SWFs are a metamorphosis of state–run businesses. The opportunities in the contemporary global political economy are different from those in the past. Domestic economies, modes of trade, and global governance have evolved. States have learned from their past entrepreneurial experience. The liberalization of financial markets and technological advancements have made the real–time flow of information and capital among states possible. All these changes call for a new entrepreneurial paradigm. As Cerny rightly puts it, "[d]omestic sources of inputs and domestic markets for products are too small to be economically efficient."[34]

Entrepreneur states have learned not only about new opportunities but about new instruments as well. They have become more creative in managing their resources to make profit. As rational economic agents, they conduct a cost–benefit analysis with respect to the holding of assets, which include both natural resources and financial instruments. They have also become more sophisticated in their methods of dealing with structural uncertainty. They tend to incorporate inter–temporal variables more systematically into their political decisions. For instance, in the case of Saudi Arabia, "the Kingdom faces a choice between extracting or preserving oil reserves. Amongst the many complex and interlinked factors influencing this choice is the rate of return available on reinvesting the proceeds of extracted oil."[35] In other words, the Saudis are conducting an inter–temporal cost–benefit analysis, as a part of assets and risk management. The question they

---

32   Robert Wade, "The Role of Government in Overcoming Market Failure: Taiwan, Republic of Korea and Japan," in *Achieving Industrialization in East Asia*, ed. Helen Hughes (Cambridge: Cambridge University Press, 1988); ———, "State Intervention In "Outward–Looking" Development: Neoclassical Theory and Taiwanese Practice," in *Developmental States in East Asia*, ed. Gordon White (New York: St. Martin's Press, 1988); ———, *Governing the Market* (Princeton, N.J.: Princeton University Press, 1990).

33   Pier Angelo Toninelli, "The Rise and Fall of Public Enterprise: The Framework," in *The Rise and Fall of State-Owned Enterprise in the Western World*, ed. Pier Angelo Toninelli (Cambridge University Press, 2000), 10.

34   Philip G. Cerny, "The Competition State Today: From *Raison d'État* to *Raison du Monde*," *Policy Studies* 31, no. 1 (2010).

35   "The Global Oil Market: A Long–Term Perspective," (Samba Financial Group, 2008), 8.

are faced with is whether to extract oil today and invest the proceeds in a well–diversified portfolio with a long–term stream of profits, or alternatively, preserve the oil and extract it gradually over time.

While making such decisions is more complicated by the reality of intervening factors, e.g., domestic politics, policy dynamics within the OPEC, and the dynamics of the global political economy, nevertheless, this kind of analysis is crucial to state entrepreneurship. Learning, in addition to analysis and planning, is another entrepreneurial quality. Again in the case of Saudi Arabia, the state had learned from the Norwegian case that extracting oil and transforming it into a well–diversified international portfolio of equities can help increase the return on the assets and minimize risks.[36]

It is, therefore, possible for states to act as an independent entrepreneur to increase earnings and manage financial risks. States define and assess their assets, identify opportunities (both domestic and global) and take advantage of those opportunities. States have realized the increasing intangibility of value. Some have established the institutions of virtual states and learned how to use advanced technology, and focus on "creative and management services, [and] designing new products."[37] They have discovered what Cerny calls the "infrastructure of the infrastructure," i.e., the financialization of states' core processes.[38] Their domestic markets are too small to be economically efficient and profitable. Therefore, investment is flowed into states with well–established and functioning markets.

Entrepreneurship not only involves identification of opportunities but also extracting profit from those opportunities. Moreover, entrepreneurship involves planning, learning, and innovation, and many states, including those with SWFs have been shown to possess those qualities and to act accordingly, i.e., maximize their earnings while managing financial risks.

Domestic Compensation

The domestic compensation argument can also provide an explanation as to why some states have chosen to establish SWFs. States have different motives for providing compensation. Additionally, methods, scale, and the beneficiaries of compensation are not the same for all states. One of the arguments that speaks to the necessity of domestic compensation is drawn upon what Ruggie calls embedded liberalism compromise, a mediation between market and society. It is an economic order that is a function of social variables, with the role of state redefined as being

---

36   Ibid.

37   Richard N. Rosecrance, *The Rise of the Virtual State: Wealth and Power in the Coming Century* (New York: Basic Books, 1999), 23.

38   Philip G. Cerny, "The Infrastructure of the Infrastructure? Toward 'Embedded Financial Orthodoxy' in the International Political Economy," in *Transcending the State-Global Divide: The Neoconstructuralist Agenda in International Relations*, ed. Barry Gills and Ronen Palan (Boulder, Colo.: Lynne Reiner, 1994).

the safeguarding of society from downward pressure on wages, low productivity, and growing foreign competition, and at the same time, instituting self–regulating markets.[39] According to Ruggie, the success of post–war economic liberalization was made possible by a "compact between state and society to mediate its deleterious domestic effects."[40]

In the post–war era, barriers to trade and capital flow were torn down, as a result of both dominant liberal ideas and shifts in domestic politics. According to Milner and Kubota, political leaders may also have lowered trade barriers or pursued international economic liberalization policies as a strategy for building domestic political support. Groups that gained from these policies tended to be powerful supporters of the leaders: "democratic political competition meant that leaders were likely to liberalize trade to appeal to these new groups to ensure their political survival."[41]

Geddes maintains that economic liberalization can be very costly, especially for "fragile, uninstitutionalized new democracies ... [where] its costs make it unpopular and hence politically suicidal to elected officials."[42] This means political leaders may need to provide compensation in order to ensure the political stability. Liberalizing state may have established SWFs to accumulate and manage resources for domestic compensation.

A second argument that is relevant to domestic compensation perspective is the problem of smallness. Smallness is an issue because "[b]y their very nature, small states are exposed to economic, political and environmental forces which may greatly amplify the fluctuations in their growth with disproportionate impact relative to larger countries."[43] Large industrial states have the option of exporting or avoiding costs of economic change in times of hardship. Still, as Katzenstein puts it, "[i]n the global economy the odds are stacked against small and dependent states."[44] SWFs in states like United Arab Emirates, Kuwait, Norway, or Singapore can provide some means of protection against the problem of "smallness."

---

39   John Gerard Ruggie, "International Regimes, Transactions and Change: Embedded Liberalism in the Postwar Economic Order," *International Organization* 36 (1982).

40   ———, "Globalization and the Embedded Liberalism Compromise: The End of an Era?," *MPIfG Working Paper* 97/1(1997).

41   Helen V. Milner and Keiko Kubota, "Why the Move to Free Trade? Democracy and Trade Policy in the Developing Countries," *International Organization* 59, (2005). 113.

42   Barbara Geddes, "Challenging the Conventional Wisdom," in *Economic Reform and Democracy*, ed. Larry Diamond and Marc Plattner (Baltimore, Md.: Johns Hopkins University Press, 1995).

43   Harvey W. Armstrong and Robert Read, "The Phantom of Liberty?: Economic Growth and the Vulnerability of Small States," *Journal of International Development* 14(2002): 441.

44   Peter J. Katzenstein, *Small States in World Markets: Industrial Policy in Europe*, Cornell Studies in Political Economy (Ithaca, N.Y.: Cornell University Press, 1985), 36.

The third view under the domestic compensation is the resource curse argument. The majority of scholars, especially in developmental economics, contend that the resource curse argument can be used to explain why countries that export minimally processed natural resources—including petroleum and minerals—usually do not perform as well as resource–poor countries. One way of compensating for the loss of the natural resources that are a part of national wealth is through the efficient management of the proceeds from their export. Some political economy scholars attribute the poor performance of resource–abundant states to the rent–seeking behavior of the governments of natural resource–exporting states.[45] Additionally, governments in the resource–abundant states rely mostly on the revenues from the export of natural resources rather than on domestic sources, i.e., taxes. SWFs can certainly provide the vehicle for the preservation of the value of non–renewable resources, and reduce the governments' dependance on internal sources of income (taxes). Interestingly, the list of states with sovereign wealth funds represents a good number of resource–abundant states, with low tax–based economies, including the United Arab Emirates, Kuwait, Qatar, Oman, Russia, Iran, and Kazakhstan.

It is, however, important to note that there are major conceptual differences between the various types of domestic compensation. The domestic compensation argument can reflect three reasons for wealth redistribution from the standpoint of domestic politics. First, political leaders may need to provide compensation to their constituencies (voters or supporters of the political regime) in order to ensure the continuity of their governments; second, the governments may need resources in order to manage macroeconomic deficiencies including redressing the fiscal deficit; and third, the governments may find it necessary to diversify the industrial base of the domestic economy. The type of compensation in the first instance is more likely to be corrupt in the case of non–democratic states, while managing macroeconomic deficiencies or diversifying the industrial base arguably involves the more legitimate goal of providing public goods. A concern related to the politics of domestic compensation is that the less transparent funds may be engaged in corrupt compensation practices.

The various theoretical perspectives discussed earlier, not only help expand our understanding of the creation and operation of SWFs, but also lead us to critical questions that we should ask when assessing a sovereign fund. These questions are discussed in more details in the next section.

---

45   For more information see: Hussein Mahdavy, "The Patterns and Problems of Economic Development in Rentier States: The Case of Iran," in *Studies in Economic History of the Middle East*, ed. M. A. Cook (London: Oxford University Press, 1970); Kiren Aziz Chaudhry, "The Price of Wealth: Business and State in Labor Remittance and Oil Economies," *International Organization* 43, (1989); ———, "Economic Liberalization and the Lineage of the Rentier State," *Comparative Politics* 27, (1994).

Asking the Right Question

After reviewing key characteristics of SWFs and various theoretical perspectives that can explain the creation and functioning of SWFs and hence unique features of the funds, we can now formulate questions based on which one can evaluate the real agenda and behavior of the funds. There are, however, a few points that I wish to highlight.

First, as mentioned earlier, the purpose of a fund does not necessarily remain the same but may change over time. The agenda of a fund, set in the 1950s or 1970s, for instance, can be less relevant today. This is because over time, countries undergo structural changes in their modes of production, demography, society, and in some cases, even the political system. Globalization has also made domestic transformation inevitable. The other reason why an old agenda may not be relevant today is that political and economic changes on both the global and domestic levels change the shape and nature of a country's interdependency with the outside world over time. Therefore, the proper approach in the study of SWFs would be to look at them longitudinally, and not at a single point in time.

Second, all of the theoretical perspectives discussed earlier can be applied to a fund, depending on the period being considered. Many states such as Norway and Russia, introduced economic stimulus plans when faced with the global economic downturn. They increased government expenditures, which was partially financed through their SWFs or resources that would have otherwise been deposited to their funds. So at times of economic hardship, sovereign funds act similarly and according to domestic compensation thesis. At times of economic prosperity, on the other hand, we would expect the governments to adopt a higher risk–taking threshold. The governments can become aggressive capitalist entrepreneurs with the goal of achieving highest return. They may also invest (or divest) in areas and industries as they see fit, based on their political agenda or foreign policy goals, if any.

What this tells us is that SWFs are theoretically progressive. More importantly, while various funds may show similar behavior at times of economic contraction, it is the times of prosperity that can really tell us what the differences are between the various funds. Therefore, in order to ascertain the main differences between the funds, more attention should be paid to periods of normal or booming economic activity.

Lastly, while a particular goal might be of great importance at some point, it might subsequently lose its prominence as a result of changes in institutional or external factors, such as changes in a state's priorities or shifts in the global economy. The SWFs' goals can also be multiple, changing, or even overlapping, in which case the critical question to ask is how the owner states balance their various goals against each other.

In order to determine which of the three theoretical perspectives prevails in explaining different stages during the life of a SWF—hence determining what the real agenda of the fund is—I introduce a number of key markers or qualifying questions. These markers are summarized in Appendix I. When assessing the behavior of SWFs, there are three main areas we need to look at. The first one is the structure of the fund's management and its relationship with the government. The second area is the behavior of the fund, and more specifically, the fund's actual investment; and the third one is the environment (domestic or international) in which the state and their sovereign funds operate.

As discussed earlier, the realists explain the creation of SWFs in terms of state's power calculation. If so, then we would expect to observe a close relationship between the fund's management and the political leaders, and therefore, state's policies. [46] That means changes in political leadership would result in changes in the fund's agenda. This also means that the fund management does not enjoy independence from the political apparatus in their financial and investment decision making but takes directives from the political leaders whether directly or in the form of some rules and regulations. In cases like this, it is also likely to see political leaders, in their statements, refer to the fund as a means of statecraft or foreign policy tool. Such statements are also indications of the political purpose of the funds.

In addition to the management and its relationship with the political administration, the actual investment approach of the SWFs can also give us an indication about the real agenda of the fund. Investment in politically sensitive industries such as defense is not so much in tune with the goal of domestic compensation or risk–return optimization goal. Investment in areas that are not commercially sound also raises a red flag and questions the real agenda of the fund. After all, no rational economic actor or state, whether for the purpose of managing the value of its reserves or national savings, would invest in areas that are financially unsound or excessively risky.

SWFs that are managed according to principles of risk–return optimization and constantly react to movements in the markets are more likely to indicate the state entrepreneurship or domestic compensation goals of the states. In such cases, the funds are more likely managed by professional fund managers or external managers. States that have historically intervened in the economy—especially at times when domestic markets lacked efficient economic actors—or have established state–owned enterprises (SOEs), are more likely to have established sovereign funds. SWFs, as a manifestation of state entrepreneurship, are expected to manage national wealth efficiently and so we would expect them to act somewhat similar to private financial institutions, i.e., manage the portfolio actively and

---

46   The key here is the relationship between the fund's manager and the government. Where the fund itself is located (in terms of state's administrative structure) may not be as important since the fund can be formally within a specific administration or ministry (as most of the funds are) but operate under minimal direct supervision by political leaders or have independent decision making processes so that the investment decisions are not affected by internal politics.

with sophistication, optimize risk and profit, and respond to movements in global markets.[47]

States that pursue the goal of maximizing the value of their reserves—those separate from official reserves held by the central bank—tend to have a portfolio that consists of risky assets. A portfolio that contains more risky assets (equities) than low–risk fixed–income instruments (bonds or treasury bills) also indicates a higher risk tolerance (and therefore possibility for higher returns) compared to conservative or precautionary funds. For entrepreneurial states, this is an ongoing and dynamic process that involves continuous learning, adaptation, and sometimes speculations.

Additional qualifying questions can help identify SWFs that were created for domestic compensation purposes. States that are small and open to internal trade are also vulnerable to external market shocks. These states can use their SWFs to manage resources needed during times of economic crisis. Another marker— mainly applicable to developed and open democracies—is the existence of an efficient domestic redistribution mechanism that can funnel the proceeds from sovereign fund investment abroad to the society. In these countries, the domestic compensation is intended for the entire society and is channeled through social safety nets and various redistribution mechanisms.

In the case of non–democratic states that generally lack an efficient system of taxation, SWFs can provide resources for funding governments' expenditures. Inefficient or non–existing taxation system means that the government has to rely on external sources of income for budgetary purposes. Additionally, SWFs whose accounts are integrated in national budgets are more likely to be used for domestic compensation as the governments tend to rely more on the resources of the fund for their budgetary purposes.

As mentioned earlier, the three theoretical perspectives may share traits. Therefore, some of these markers or qualifying questions can be applied to multiple perspectives. For instance, states whose SWF is aimed at domestic compensation, may still have independent or external managers. However, if a country is small, open, or resource–abundant—and in general vulnerable to external shocks—it is more likely that it has established a SWF for domestic compensation purposes. Additionally, if the SWF's account is integrated into the national budget and is drawn upon on various occasions, for instance for pension payments or financing government expenditures, it well may be the case that the SWFs' assets are used for domestic purposes rather than the pursuit of political power. In the next four chapters, I will apply these questions to selected case studies in order to determine the purpose of the selected funds according to the international political economic perspectives discussed earlier.

---

47   States with entrepreneurial skills and spirit allow their SWFs to engage in sophisticated, and sometimes complex, transactions such as mergers and acquisitions, and indirect investments.

Before proceeding with the case studies, we need to briefly discuss a main assumption under which we can apply the qualifying questions and assess the purpose of the fund. The economic well–being of the owner states has an impact on the immediate agenda of the fund. States, when faces with extreme external pressures such as market crashes or prolonged global recession, may exhaust all domestic sources and temporarily abandon the main goal of the SWF, and thus divert the fund's resources for coping with economic hardship. In other words, at times of economic austerity, states' priorities shift towards managing domestic economic problems. At times of prosperity or normal economic activity, however, states are not financially constrained, and thus, can pursue their real agenda through their SWFs. For the purpose of this study, the recent global financial crisis provides an excellent opportunity—with a comparable extent and impact among many states—to observe the changes in the performance of the funds. As will be shown, states discussed in this book either directly withdraw upon their SWFs resources or reduce their contribution to the funds. At the time of normal activity, each of these funds was shown to have pursued different goals. The history, management, and performance of the selected SWFs along with the environment in which they function are discussed in more details in the next four chapters.

References

Armstrong, Harvey W., and Robert Read. "The Phantom of Liberty?: Economic Growth and the Vulnerability of Small States." *Journal of International Development* 14 (2002): 435-58.

Baldwin, David A. *Economic Statecraft*. Princeton, N.J.: Princeton University Press, 1985.

Beck, Roland, and Michael Fidora. "The Impact of Sovereign Wealth Funds on Global Financial Markets." European Central Bank, 2008.

Butt, Shams, Anil Shivdasani, Carsten Stendevad, and Ann Wyman. "Sovereign Wealth Funds: A Growing Global Force in Corporate Finance." *Journal of Applied Corporate Finance* 20, no. 1 (2008): 73-83.

Cerny, Philip G. "The Competition State Today: From *Raison d'État* to *Raison du Monde*." *Policy Studies* 31, no. 1 (2010): 5-21.

———. "The Infrastructure of the Infrastructure? Toward 'Embedded Financial Orthodoxy' in the International Political Economy." In *Transcending the State-Global Divide: The Neoconstructuralist Agenda in International Relations*, edited by Barry Gills and Ronen Palan, 251-74. Boulder, Colo.: Lynne Reiner, 1994.

Chaudhry, Kiren Aziz. "Economic Liberalization and the Lineage of the Rentier State." *Comparative Politics* 27 (1994).

———. "The Price of Wealth: Business and State in Labor Remittance and Oil Economies." *International Organization* 43 (1989).

Cohn, Theodore H. *Global Political Economy : Theory and Practice*. 2nd ed. New York: Longman, 2003.

Eisinger, Peter K. *The Rise of the Entrepreneurial State: State and Local Economic Development Policy in the United States*, La Follette Public Policy Series. Madison, Wis.: University of Wisconsin Press, 1988.

Farrell, Diana, and Susan Lund. "The New Role of Oil Wealth in the World Economy." *McKinsey Quarterly* January (2008).

Geddes, Barbara. "Challenging the Conventional Wisdom." In *Economic Reform and Democracy*, edited by Larry Diamond and Marc Plattner, 59-73. Baltimore, Md.: Johns Hopkins University Press, 1995.

Gilpin, Robert. *Global Political Economy of International Relations*. Princeton: Princeton University Press, 1987.

"The Global Oil Market: A Long–Term Perspective." Samba Financial Group, 2008.

Griffith-Jones, Stephany, and José Antonio Ocampo. *Sovereign Wealth Funds: A Developing Country Perspective*, Workshop on Sovereign Wealth Funds. London: Andean Development Corporation 2008.

Haskel, Barbara. "Access to Society: A Neglected Dimension of Power." *International Organization* 34, no. 1 (1980): 89-120.

Hirschman, Albert O. *National Power and the Structure of Foreign Trade*. Berkeley and Los Angeles: University of California Press, 1945.

Katzenstein, Peter J. *Small States in World Markets: Industrial Policy in Europe*, Cornell Studies in Political Economy. Ithaca, N.Y.: Cornell University Press, 1985.

Kern, Steffen. "Sovereign Wealth Funds–State Investments on the Rise." Deutsche Bank, 2007.

Kimmit, R.M. "Public Footprints in Private Markets." Foreign Affairs 87, no. 1 (2008).

Kirzner, Israel M. *Competition and Entrepreneurship*. Chicago: University of Chicago Press, 1973.

———. *Discovery and the Capitalist Process*. Chicago: University of Chicago Press, 1985.

———. *Perception, Opportunity, and Profit: Studies in the Theory of Entrepreneurship*. Chicago: University of Chicago Press, 1979.

Luedde-Neurath, Richard. "State Intervention and Export–Oriented Development in South Korea." In *Developmental States in East Asia*, edited by Gordon White. New York: St. Martin's Press, 1988.

Lyons, Gerard. "State Capitalism: The Rise of Sovereign Wealth Funds." Standard Chartered Bank, 2007.

Mahdavy, Hussein. "The Patterns and Problems of Economic Development in Rentier States: The Case of Iran." In *Studies in Economic History of the Middle East*, edited by M. A. Cook. London: Oxford University Press, 1970.

Milner, Helen V., and Keiko Kubota. "Why the Move to Free Trade? Democracy and Trade Policy in the Developing Countries." *International Organization* 59, no. Winter 2005 (2005): 107-43.

Rosecrance, Richard N. *The Rise of the Virtual State: Wealth and Power in the Coming Century*. New York: Basic Books, 1999.

Ruggie, John Gerard. "Globalization and the Embedded Liberalism Compromise: The End of an Era?" *MPIfG Working Paper* 97/1 (1997).

———. "International Regimes, Transactions and Change: Embedded Liberalism in the Postwar Economic Order." *International Organization* 36 (1982): 379-415.

Schumpeter, Joseph. *Capitalism, Socialism and Democracy*. New York: Harper and Row, 1962.

"Sovereign Wealth Fund Institute." http://swfinstitute.org/.

"Sovereign Wealth Funds–a Work Agenda." International Monetary Fund, 2008.

Strange, Susan. *States and Markets*. New York: Basil Blackwell, 1988.

The United States Senate Committee on Banking, Housing and Urban Affairs. *Testimony of Edwin M. Truman, Senior Fellow, Peterson Institute for International Economics*, 14 November 2007.

Thucydides. *The History of the Peloponnesian War*. New York: Dutton, 1910.

Toninelli, Pier Angelo. "The Rise and Fall of Public Enterprise: The Framework." In *The Rise and Fall of State-Owned Enterprise in the Western World*, edited by Pier Angelo Toninelli: Cambridge University Press, 2000.

Truman, Edwin M. "A Scoreboard for Sovereign Wealth Funds." In *Conference on China's Exchange Rate Policy*. Washington D.C.: Peterson Institute for International Economics, 2007.

Wade, Robert. *Governing the Market*. Princeton, N.J.: Princeton University Press, 1990.

———. "The Role of Government in Overcoming Market Failure: Taiwan, Republic of Korea and Japan." In *Achieving Industrialization in East Asia*, edited by Helen Hughes. Cambridge: Cambridge University Press, 1988.

———. "State Intervention In "Outward–Looking" Development: Neoclassical Theory and Taiwanese Practice." In *Developmental States in East Asia*, edited by Gordon White. New York: St. Martin's Press, 1988.

Yu, Tony F. "Entrepreneurial State: The Role of Government in the Economic Development of the Asian Newly Industrialising Economies." *Development Policy Review* 15 (1997): 47-64.

Chapter 3
How Norway's Government Pension Fund–Global Conducts Foreign Policy

The Government Pension Fund–Global (GPF–Global) of Norway is one of the world's largest SWFs, with total assets under management of 2,763 billion krone[1] (approximately $441 billion) as of the end of March 2010. The GPF–Global is one of the most transparent funds. The history of the fund dates back to more than two decades ago. As will be shown, the fund has been pursuing different goals over its lifetime. At the beginning, the GPF–Global mission was to provide necessary resources for meeting the government's future pension obligations. The GPF–Global has also provided financial support to the government at times of economic contraction, or large budget deficits.

Years after its creation, the fund's management started to make investment decisions according to a set of non–economic guidelines, which are expressions of the Norwegian national political consensus. As will be discussed, the purely economic view is not a relevant framework for explaining active ownership motivated by the ideal of socially–responsible investment, or sanctioning investment in areas that are in contradiction to the fund's Ethical Guidelines. In fact, the Norwegian foreign policy agenda, encapsulated in the Guidelines, determines where investments (or divestments) would be made.

In this chapter, I will first start with a discussion of the economic and political circumstances that have led to the creation of the GPF–Global. I will show that the creation of GPF–Global was preceded by an external economic shock (first oil crisis), a massive current account deficit, and the recognition that the existing structure for funding future public pension obligations was inadequate. I will then discuss the current status of the fund and will review the fund's present portfolio structure and performance. I will also identify periods of economic hardship or financial crises and discuss the role (if any) played by the Norwegian SWF in smoothing the external shocks to the economy or easing the pressures on national budget or balance of payments. As will be shown, at times of economic contraction, the Norwegian government has relied on GPF–Global as a source of relief for the domestic economy.

During periods of normal activity and in the absence of financial constraints, however, the fund's investment decisions and management reflected the actual agenda of the fund, which was more in line with the economic statecraft argument.

---

1   "Government Pension Fund–Global, First Quarter 2010," (Oslo: Norges Bank Investment Management, 2010).

For instance, GPF–Global started to incorporate non–commercial and somewhat political factors into its decision making as early as 2004. In fact its involvement in political contests began with its involvement in an oil company in Africa and the related disputes.

As discussed in the previous chapter, a SWF may have several goals on its agenda. The case study of the Norwegian SWF identifies various objectives of the GPF–Global. The chapter will conclude with the assertion that the GPF–Global has in fact pursued various objectives including economic statecraft but not in its traditional form. The Norwegian government has used the GPF–Global, on many occasions, to communicate its political preferences with the target state or companies through negative screening or sanctioning of investment in certain areas.

Born Out of Foresight

The history of the GPF–Global as well as its source of funding is closely related to the petroleum sector. Therefore, a brief history of the Norwegian petroleum industry is relevant. In 1963, Norway proclaimed its sovereignty over the continental shelf and begun the exploration and exploitation of submarine natural resources. The Statoil (the state oil company) was established in 1972. Only a year later and before the country could extract profit from the petroleum sector, Norway was hit by the first oil crisis. Gasoline was rationed, car–free days were introduced, and Norway's King Olav took the tram. The Statfjord field was discovered in the North Sea in 1974, but production from this field started only in 1979 and the Statoil became the sole operator of the field in 1981.[2]

The second oil crisis created a recession in most developed countries, but not in Norway—an oil exporter—that had focused on the petroleum sector. Heavy reliance on oil, however, had its own downside. Norway gradually lost its international market competitiveness and experienced de–industrialization, a phenomenon commonly known as Dutch Disease. In the early 1980s, while liberalization and privatization were occurring in many other countries, the conservative government of Norway continued to heavily regulate the economy, going so far as to have the Storting (the Parliament) setting the interest rates at a much lower rate than the market level.[3] When oil prices fell dramatically in December 1985, the artificially–produced economic prosperity of the mid–1980s could no longer be sustained and Norway experienced a huge deficit.[4] Norway

---

2   "The Norwegian Oil History," Norwegian Petroleum Directorate (Oljedirektoratet), http://www.npd.no/English/Om+OD/Nyttig/Olje-ABC/Norsk+oljehistorie/70_tallet.htm.

3   Ola Grytten, "The Economic History of Norway," in *EH.Net Encyclopedia*, ed. Robert Whaples (2008).

4   The average crude oil price fell about 48 percent from $27 in 1985 to $14 per barrel in 1986. The current account balance that had a $3 billion surplus in 1985 experienced a

managed to correct the current account deficit after almost three years. Since 1989 Norway has continuously sustained a current account surplus. The current account surplus has been more than 12 percent of the GDP, reaching 16.4 percent in 2006, the highest point in the last decade.[5] Today, Norway is the world's fourth largest exporter of oil (after Saudi Arabia, Russia, and Iran) and the third largest exporter of gas (after Russia and Canada).[6]

It took Norway almost two decades to realize that the oil reserves are not available indefinitely. For long, it was believed that the oil and gas reserves in the Norwegian shelf were to be depleted as early as 2015.[7] It was only in June 2009 that Royal Dutch Shell, Europe's largest petroleum company, announced that it had made a natural gas discovery 360 kilometers (224 miles) offshore Brønnøysund in the northern Norwegian Sea.[8]

On 22 June 1990, the Storting passed the Government Petroleum Fund Act in order to support the long–term management of proceeds from the oil revenues. The Oljefondet (the Petroleum Fund) was established the same year; however, the first net transfer to the fund took place only in 1996. Between 1998 and 2002, equities and non–government bonds were also added to the fund's portfolio. On 21 December 2005, the Storting passed the Government Pension Fund Act to "support central government saving to finance the National Insurance Scheme's expenditure on pensions and long–term consideration in the application of petroleum revenues."[9] As a result, the Government Petroleum Fund Act of 1990 was repealed. On 1 January 2006, the Government Pension Fund was established, indicating its mission as supporting a "broader pension reform, highlighting also the fund's role in facilitating government savings necessary to meet the rapid rise in public pension expenditures in the coming years."[10] The GPF–Global was in fact one of two funds that were created under the umbrella of the Government Pension Fund for the management of the latter's foreign assets.

The other fund was the Government Pension Fund–Norway (GPN–Norway), which managed the domestic assets of the Government Pension Fund. Under the 2005 Act, the responsibility of managing both GPF–Global and GPF–Norway rests with the Ministry of Finance. The operational management of the GPF–

---

deficit of $4.5 billion in 1986.

5   "External Trade in Commodities," Statistics Norway, http://www.ssb.no.

6   "The World Fact Book," CIA, https://www.cia.gov/library/publications/the-world-factbook/docs/rankorderguide.html.

7   "OLF the Norwegian Oil Industry Association," http://www.olf.no/about-olf/category292.html.

8   Marianne Stigset, "Shell Gas Find in Norway May Be Biggest in 12 Years," *Bloomberg*, 19 June 2009.

9   "Provisions on the Management of the Government Pension Fund," (Ministry of Finance, Government of Norway), 7.

10   "Background Note: Norway's Position in Relation to the International Debate on Sovereign Wealth Funds," (Asset Management Department, The Norwegian Ministry of Finance, 2007), 7.

Global has, however, been delegated to Norges Bank (the Norwegian Central Bank), while Folketrygdfondet[11] has been managing the daily operations of the GPF–Norway.[12] The GPF–Global accounted for 95 percent of the overall value of the Government Pension Fund at the end of the first half of 2008, while the GPF–Norway accounted for the remaining 5 percent.[13] Figure 3.1 presents a timeline of the evolution of the fund.

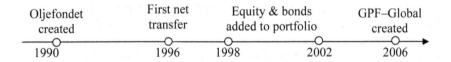

Figure 3.1   Timeline of the evolution of the Norwegian SWF

Both GPF–Global and GPF–Norway's major objective is to generate a higher return than the benchmark over time, within the defined risk margin, with the goal of "safeguarding the basis of future welfare, including national pension."[14] Norges Bank and Folketrygdfondet exploit their defined risk margin by investing in securities that fall outside of the scope of the benchmark portfolio while investing other portions of the fund in certain securities set by the benchmark portfolio in order to achieve returns in excess of the returns on benchmark portfolio.[15]

Although the GPF–Global is the official Sovereign Wealth Fund of Norway, the period of study here will not be confined to the short period of 2006 and after. On the other hand, 1990 would not be the most appropriate starting point, as until 1996 the Oljefondet existed only on paper. Between 1996 and 1998, when it received some of the petroleum sector income, Oljefondet was more of a saving fund. It was only after 1998 that equities and non–government bonds were gradually added to the portfolio of the fund. Therefore, 1998 is a more relevant starting point. Where the fund stands today is the focus of the next section.

---

11   Folketrygdfondet is a company by special statute, with the Norwegian state as the sole owner. It manages the Government Pension Fund–Norway, with assets under it management of 113 billion krone at the end of 2007. For more information see http://www. ftf.no/about_ftf.html.

12   The Government Pension Fund–Norway is invested in equities and fixed–income vehicles of Norway (85 percent of the benchmark portfolio), as well as in Denmark, Finland and Sweden (15 percent of the benchmark portfolio).

13   "Chapter 5: The Management of the Government Pension Fund," in *National Budget 2009* (Ministry of Finance, Government of Norway), 4.

14   Norges Bank website (www.norges–bank.no).

15   "Chapter 5: The Management of the Government Pension Fund," 3.

GPF–Global, Today

The petroleum sector and activities related to this industry are the main source of funding of the GPF–Global. Other sources of cash flow are the fund's own return on investment and the net result of financial transactions associated with the petroleum sector. The Norwegian Ministry of Finance acts as the owner of the fund and reports on all matters related to the fund's performance to the Norwegian Storting. The operational management of the fund is delegated by the Ministry of Finance to the Norges Bank Investment Management (NBIM).[16] A management agreement defines the relationship between the Ministry of Finance (as the delegating authority) and Norges Bank (as the operational manager).[17]

The GPF–Global is managed partially by Norges Bank and partially by external managers. However, the key management strategy is dictated by the Ministry of Finance. The Ministry of Finance sets the long–term investment strategy by defining the structure of the "benchmark portfolio," in accordance with the general consensus in the Storting, with regard to objective of high–return subject to moderate–risk. "The long term investment horizon of the fund means that the portions invested in various asset classes and geographical regions can be determined on the basis of the assessment of expected long–term returns and risks."[18]

Norges Bank has to follow the benchmark portfolio closely, although it has been given some leeway. The Ministry of Finance has established the limits within which the expected return on the actual investment can deviate from the expected return on the benchmark portfolio.[19] The structure of the benchmark portfolio determines 90 to 95 percent of the actual portfolio return.

In January 1998, when the Oljefondet started to invest in the equity market, Norges Bank hired the first external manager. The first active equity mandates were set in December that year. For fixed–income mandates, external managers were hired in April 2000 and after.[20] The external managers were selected by looking

---

16　NBIM is one of four wings of the Norges Bank with three main areas of responsibilities including, managing the foreign currency portfolio of the GPF–Global (on behalf of the Ministry of Finance), managing the foreign currency portfolio of the Government Petroleum Insurance fund (on behalf of the Ministry of Petroleum and Energy), and managing Norges Bank's long–term portfolio of foreign exchange reserves. Source: Norges Bank website (http://www.norges–bank.no/templates/article_49384.aspx).

17　"Government Pension Fund–Global," Norges Bank, http://www.norges-bank.no/.

18　"Chapter 5: The Management of the Government Pension Fund," 2.

19　The Ministry of Finance uses the 'expected tracking error' (ETE) as a risk measure to manage the market risk of the fund. The ETE is defined as the expected value of the standard deviation of the difference between the annual return on actual investment and annual return on the benchmark portfolio. The Ministry has limited the ETE to 1.5 percentage points, meaning that in two out of three years, the fund's return should not deviate from the return on the benchmark portfolio by more than 1.5 percentage points.

20　"Government Pension Fund–Global."

at characteristics such as their information advantage, portfolio composition, and portfolio implementation methods. Norges Bank has continued to hire external managers. The amount of assets managed by the external managers as a proportion of total fund assets was 11 percent as of June 2008 (the lowest level since equities were introduced in 1998), and rose to 13.5 percent by the end of September 2008 but fell again to about 12 percent at the end of 2009. The GPF–Global may be considered a role model with respect to transparency and information disclosure. The management of the fund is characterized by a relatively high degree of transparency, information disclosure, and professionalism. At the international level, the GPF–Global actively participated in the International Working Group, sponsored by the IMF in May 2008, and contributed to the preparation of a set of voluntary guidelines referred to as the Generally Accepted Principles and Practices (GAPP), also known as the Santiago Principles.[21]

At the national level, Norges Bank (as GPF–Global manger) is required to report the results of its performance to the Ministry of Finance on a quarterly basis. In each Quarterly Report, Norges Bank provides an overall market review, a discussion of portfolio adjustments and changes in its market value, and associated risk and return figures. The report also provides updates on other issues, including those pertaining to corporate governance and the exercise of ownership rights, socially–responsible investments (including those related to sustainable development, environmental protection, and fight against child labor). The quarterly and annual reports are available to the public through the Norges Bank website.

The Ministry of Finance also uses Mercer Investment Consulting to verify the performance of Norges Bank in a more detailed and technical manner. The GPF–Global is also subject to audits by the Office of the Auditor General (OAG) or Riksrevisjonen.[22] This office has agreed with Norges Bank to follow the audit approach employed by the Norges Bank Auditing Department. In 2007, the Ministry of Finance announced that it would hold a public hearing on amendments to the accounting and auditing clauses of the Central Bank Act to enhance controls and supervisions. The Ministry has also maintained that the increased complexity of the management of the GPF–Global, together with the increase in its assets, calls for measures beyond those designated by the internal audit department or

21   Santiago Principles or Generally Accepted Principles and Practices (GAPP) for Sovereign Wealth Funds are the product of the International Working Group (IWG) of SWFs, which was established on 1 May 2008. The IWG was tasked to prepare a set of voluntary principles that would promote a better understanding of the issues related to SWFs, including their institutional framework, governance and transparency. The IWG presented the Santiago Principles, a set of 24 voluntary principles, to the IMF on 11 October 2008.

22   The Office of the Auditor General (OAG) or *Riksrevisjonen* is the Norwegian state's auditor, under and reporting to the Storting. The OAG conducts financial audits, performance audits, and corporate control. For more information on OGA see http://www.riksrevisjonen.no/en/. The OAG has served as an external auditor for organizations such as the Permanent Council of the Organization for Security and Co–operation in Europe (OSCE) in 2006.

support from the auditing firm Deloitte, which has been within the framework of the Central Bank Act.[23]

According to section two of the Regulations on Management of the GPF–Global, the fund is placed on a separate account held with the Norges Bank and denominated in Norwegian krone. The capital is then invested—in Norges Bank's name—in financial instruments and cash deposits denominated in foreign currency. Norges Bank "shall seek to achieve the highest possible return on the investments in foreign currency within the investment limits set out in these regulations and guidelines issued under these regulations."[24]

The fund's capital is invested in non–Norwegian financial instruments, since investment in securities by Norwegian enterprises (i.e., those with head offices in Norway) is not permitted.[25] These instruments fall into two major categories: equities and fixed–income instruments. According to the early regulations on the management of the GPF–Global, the proportion of equity instruments could vary between 30 to 50 percent while the share of fixed–income instruments could vary between 50 to 70 percent.[26] Financial instruments in the portfolio may included derivatives, commodity–based contracts, and fund units. Table 3.1 shows the allowed distribution of equity and fixed–income instruments by region.

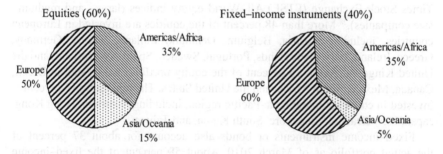

Figure 3.2   Geographical distribution of benchmark portfolio

<u>*Source*</u>: Norges Bank website

23   Specifically, the Ministry of Finance aims to hold a public hearing with regard to the following Central Bank amendments: 1) Replace the Central Bank audit arrangement by an arrangement whereby the Supervisory Council appoints an external auditor for Norges Bank; 2) Establish legal authority for regulations regarding the accounting principles Norges Bank should observe; 3) Define the scope of the audit and the content of the auditors' report. For more information see "Chapter 5: The Management of the Government Pension Fund," 10.

24   "Chapter 2: Regulations on Management of the Government Pension Fund–Global," in *Provisions on the Management of the Government Pension Fund* (Ministry of Finance, Government of Norway), Section 2.

25   Folketrygdfondet (as the operational manager of GPF–Norway) manages domestic investments.

26   "Chapter 2: Regulations on Management of the Government Pension Fund–Global," Section 4.

The most important strategic investment decision, i.e., setting the benchmark portfolio, is made by the Ministry of Finance itself. The benchmark portfolio controls the distribution of investment among various classes of assets and currencies, as well as geographical locations. Figure 3.2 shows the geographical distribution of the equities and fixed–income instruments in the benchmark portfolio.

Table 3.1   Allowed regional distribution of financial instruments (percent)

	Equity instruments	Fixed–income instruments
Europe	40–60	50–70
Americas and Africa	25–45	25–45
Asia and Oceania	5–25	0–15

Source: Section 4, Regulations on Management of the GPF–Global, Ministry of Finance

In the actual, equities account for about 62.6 percent[27] and are composed of stocks, money market instruments, and derivatives, included in the Financial Times Stock Exchange (FTSE) All–World equity indices (large– and medium–size companies).[28] More than 48 percent of the equities are invested in European countries, including Austria, Belgium, Denmark, Finland, France, Germany, Greece, Ireland, Italy, Netherlands, Portugal, Sweden, Spain, Switzerland, and the United Kingdom. About 36 percent of the equity portfolio is invested in Brazil, Canada, Mexico, South Africa, and the United States. The remaining 15 percent is invested in countries in the Asia–Pacific region, including Australia, Hong Kong, Japan, New Zealand, Singapore, South Korea, and Taiwan.

Fixed–income instruments or bonds also account for about 37 percent of the actual portfolio as of March 2010. About 58 percent of the fixed–income instruments is invested in 21 different countries and denominated in Euro, Pound Sterling, Swiss franc, Swedish krona and Danish krone.[29] Nearly 37 percent of the fixed–income instruments are invested in similar bonds in the United States and Canada, and the remaining five percent in domestic government bonds in

27   "Government Pension Fund–Global, First Quarter 2010."
28   The FTSE All–World Index Series is the Large/Mid Cap aggregate of 2,700 stocks from the FTSE Global Equity Index Series. It covers 90–95 percent of the investable market capitalization. The series is divided into Developed and Emerging segments, giving investors the opportunity to develop their own investible universe. The modular nature of the series provides maximum breadth of options for structuring portfolios with indices calculated at regional, national and sector level. For more information see: "FTSE," http://www.ftse.com/index.jsp.
29   "Government Pension Fund–Global, First Quarter 2010."

Australia, Japan, New Zealand, and Singapore. Table 3.2 provides the list of the ten largest equity and bond holdings of GPF–Global as of 31 March 2010.

Table 3.2   Largest GPF–Global holdings as of 31 March 2010 (million krone)

Equities	
Nestlé SA (Switzerland)	19,476
HSBC Holdings PLC (UK)	19,368
BP PLC (UK)	18,885
Royal Dutch Shell PLC (Netherlands)	18,747
Vodafone Group PLC (UK)	14,052
TOTAL SA (France)	13,929
Novartis AG (Switzerland)	12,722
Roche Holding AG (Switzerland)	12,335
Exxon Mobile Corp. (US)	11,978
BHP Billiton OLC (UK)	11,789
Fixed–Income Instruments	
United States	119,121
UK Government	66,863
Federal Republic of Germany	48,532
Japanese Government	43,995
French Republic	41,075
Italian Republic	39,686
European Investment Bank	21,925
Bank of Scotland PLC (UK)	20,525
Fannie Mae	17,287
Kreditanstalt für Wiederaufbau (Germany)	16,600

Source: Government Pension Fund–Global, First Quarter 2010

The return on the fund's overall portfolio in the fourth quarter of 2008 fell to −10.30 percent, the lowest point in the fund's history. The poor performance of equities contributed mainly to this overall negative performance. The fixed–income assets were primarily affected by the United States sub–prime mortgage crisis and the poor performance of the European and inflation–linked bonds. The equity section of the portfolio was also severely damaged by the losses in the United States banking sector.[30] The overall portfolio return rebound from −4.81 percent in the first quarter of 2009 to 13.51 percent in the third quarter of 2009

---

30   "Government Pension Fund–Global, Third Quarter 2008," (Oslo: Norges Bank Investment Management 2008).

(the highest quarterly return since the beginning of 2007), but fell again in the first quarter of 2010 to 3.87 percent.[31]

In Rich or Poor

In order to determine the agenda of the GPF–Global we have to assess the behavior of the fund both at times of economic contraction and economic prosperity. Let's first discuss the times of economic hardship or financial contraction. Since the creation of Oljefondet in 1990, there have been only two events that may have had a negative impact on the balance of payments of Norway. In 1998, average crude oil prices dropped by about 32 percent. The current account balance of Norway did not, however, experience a deficit, and only dropped sharply from $10 billion in 1997 to $6 million in 1998.[32] Norway managed to sustain its overall balance of payments status through the capital account that offset the downward pressure on the current account. The Oljefondet, at the time, did not seem to have played much of a role in easing the economic pressure. It is not clear why this did not happen; the government may have decided that it was not necessary to use the petroleum money, or the fund may not have had resources sufficient to support the national economy, especially since the first net transfer to the fund took place in 1996.

Drawing conclusions about the behavior of the GPF–Global (established in 2006) during periods of low oil prices is in fact impossible since the price of oil has exhibited a constant upward trend since 2006. There is, however, another kind of crisis that both the Norwegian and the global economy are exposed to—a financial crisis. Since 1990, the only financial crisis that has had a significant impact on the Norwegian economy is the recent sub–prime mortgage crisis.

The crisis began in the summer of 2007 with a fall in the value of securities backed by US sub–prime mortgages. In 2008, many large financial institutions went bankrupt or were sold to other financial institutions. Major financial institutions such as Bear Sterns, Lehman Brothers, and Merrill Lynch were already in trouble. By the end of the year, the problem had developed beyond that of a purely financial crisis, as a crisis of confidence in the financial system and a global economic downturn took hold. Governments of many industrial countries including the United States, Germany, and Japan, were forced to immediately inject money into their economies or introduce economic stimulus programs to boost employment and maintain the domestic consumption level.

The global recession did not leave Norway unaffected. On the national level, the Norwegian mainland GDP[33] had shrunken already by 0.8 percent by the end of

---

31   "Government Pension Fund–Global, Second Quarter 2009," (Oslo: Norges Bank Investment Management 2009); "Government Pension Fund–Global, First Quarter 2010."

32   International Monetary Fund., "IFS CD-ROM." (Washington, D.C.: IMF, 2009).

33   Mainland GDP refers to the GDP that excludes oil, gas, and shipping industries. Norway authorities believe mainland GDP to be a better indicator of the economic well–

the fourth quarter of 2008. The first quarter of 2009 figures showed a further one percent decline. The total GDP also shrank by 0.4 percent in the first quarter of 2009.[34] In late 2008, Jens Stoltenberg, the Norwegian prime minister, said that his government would soon announce more spending measures designed to boost the domestic economy.[35] The government announced a 20 billion krone ($2.89 billion) stimulus package that consisted of 16.75 billion krone in increased government spending with a focus on infrastructure and 3.25 billion krone in tax relief for the business sector.[36] In January 2009 the government proposed amendments to the 2009 budget. In February, it was confirmed that in the face of the global financial crisis the Norwegian government needed more financial resources in order to boost employment and protect the generous welfare–state policies. Stoltenberg, in a speech to the Confederation of Norwegian Enterprise (NHO) said:

> To counter the effects of the financial crisis, I am letting you know that in 2009 we will use much more of the oil income than is justified by the expected returns from the pension fund ... There will be extensive measures aimed at employment and welfare focused in a number of different sectors. Norway will through these measures rank among the European countries doing the most to counter the crisis.[37]

In May 2009, the government revised the national budget for 2009 and introduced the most expansionary fiscal policy in 30 years. The initial fiscal stimulus package of 0.7 percent was increased to three percent of the non–oil GDP, and the government announced that it planned to spend 130 billion krone ($20 billion) from oil revenues to tackle the global financial downturn.[38] This reflected a drastic increase in the use of oil income, which was 9.5 billion krone in 2009. Subsequently, the projections for domestic economic variables were revised. The proposal indicated the use of 39 billion krone in excess of the estimated return on the GPF–Global.

The GPF–Global itself was hit by the financial crisis. The fund's return for the fourth quarter of 2008 fell to −10.3 percent in the international currency basket. This rate of return, the lowest in the fund's history, was mainly a result of the downturn in equity markets. GPF–Global had even prepared for the bankruptcy filing by Lehman Brothers, in which the fund owned a 0.27 percent equity share

---

being because while the petroleum sector constitutes 25 percent of the economic growth, it only employs about one percent of the Norwegian labor force.

34   "Norway Enters Recession: Offical Data," *Agence France Presse*, 19 May 2009.

35   "Norway SWF Takes Domestic View," *Thomson Merger News*, 31 December 2008.

36   Elizabeth Cowley, "Oil–Rich Norway Sets Stimulus Plan," *Wall Street Journal Europe*, 27 January 2009.

37   "Norway to Dip into Oil Fund Due to Financial Crisis," *Agence France Presse*, 7 January 2009.

38   "Norway Enters Recession: Offical Data."

and 4.38 percent worth of fixed–income securities (about $840 million of stocks and bonds). Norges Bank spokeswoman, Siv Meisingseth, told the media: "This is a very serious situation which we are monitoring closely … But it is also a situation we have been prepared for."[39]

The United States mortgage market had a direct negative impact on the GPF–Global's performance. The fund held stakes in both Fannie Mae and Freddie Mac. According to Yngve Slyngstad, the fund's Chief, the total exposure amounted to 88 billion krone (about $13.36 billion). Although the amount was relatively small (less than 0.4 percent of the fund portfolio), it was significant since the fund had considered this investment "the second most secure investment in the United States."[40] Later, in November 2008, and in the face of losses due to weak equity markets, Finance Minister Halvorsen said: "This will be a hard year for the fund … this will be a year of losses, especially in the equity markets … Because we are very long term investors, we are not panicking, even if this is going to be a year of losses."[41]

As mentioned earlier, the GPF–Global is fully integrated into the national budget. The fiscal policy guidelines that Norway put in place in 2001 stipulated increasing use of the oil revenues. The government was permitted to develop a non–oil budget deficit of 4 percent (equal to the expected real return on the GPF–Global) over time. However, the guidelines had provisions for an active fiscal policy to counter economic volatility when necessary.[42]

One such event was the 2008 financial crisis, when the government had to revise the 2009 budget and propose further expansionary measures. Table 3.3 shows the Norwegian government budget for 2007 and 2008 as well as the projected 2009 figures, along with the amount of the transfers required from the GPF–Global. The table shows that the non–oil budget deficit grew by almost a factor of 10 from 2008 to 2009 and the 2009 transfer from the GPF–Global was about 14 times that required in 2008. At the time of economic hardship, the Norwegian government withdrew upon its SWF's resources to meet budgetary needs.

Table 3.3   Fiscal budget balance and GPF–Global (billion krone)

	2007	2008	2009
Non–oil budget	−1.3	−11.8	−117.6
Transfer from GPF–Global	2.8	8.4	117.6
Fiscal Budget Balance	1.5	−3.4	0.0

Source: Ministry of Finance, Norwegian Government

---

39   Wojciech Moskwa and Camilla Knudsen, "Norway's Wealth Fund Says Was Prepared for Lehman," *Reuters*, 15 September 2008.

40   Nina Berglund, "Oil Fund Takes 'Minor' Hit from U.S. Mortgage Crisis," *Aftenposten*, 26 August 2008.

41   "Norway's Oil Fund Faces Losses in 2008," *Reuters*, 10 November 2008.

42   "Press Release 48/2009: Revised National Budget 2009: Continued Expansionary Policies," (Ministry of Finance, Norway, 2009).

In summary, an examination of certain historical events preceding the creation of the fund showed that the original fund was created out of necessity and foresight, for inter–generational wealth smoothing purposes (public pension payments) and for the preservation of non–renewable resources. Over the course of almost ten years the fund evolved and it developed a new structure with a more sophisticated agenda. Hit by the recent mortgage crisis and subsequently facing the risk of recession, the government of Norway revived the wealth smoothing thesis and tapped into the GPF–Global in order to maintain a balanced budget. Conventional wisdom is that if the country is ever in need (e.g., at times of financial distress, liquidity shortage, etc.), the GPF–Global can be a source of relief for the government and the economy; and the recent events confirm this.

GPF–Global in Times of Abundance

GPF–Global has undergone several operational changes. As mentioned earlier, the major operational goal of the fund is to maximize returns on portfolio, subject to moderate risk. In doing so, GPF–Global has to follow the general structure of the benchmark portfolio set by the Ministry of Finance. The structure and weighting of the benchmark portfolio is, however, not constant; it is reviewed regularly and may be adjusted periodically as a result of changes in the market value of securities in the portfolio, or global market developments. Traditionally, 40 percent of the portfolio was made up of equities. Starting in 2007, the allocation of assets to equities has been increasing gradually to the target 60 percent.[43] With a higher equity share in the portfolio, GPF–Global is more exposed to global market volatility and risks, but at the same time, has a potentially higher return.

Another initiative by the Ministry of Finance was raising the topic of inclusion of real estate assets in the benchmark portfolio of GPF–Global in 2007. The Ministry proposed to the Storting that up to 5 percent of the capital of the fund be invested in real estate over time, with a corresponding decrease in the proportion of bonds. The Ministry outsourced the task of preparing a report, on how to formulate real estate investment strategy to Partners Group AG, a Swiss company. Starting 2010, the share of fixed–income instruments in the portfolio was reduced further by 5 percent to 35 percent, with the corresponding amount allocated to real estate.

Another significant change in the GPF–Global's investment strategy is related to the limits on holding voting shares in a single company. Initially, the fund could hold no more than 5 percent of a company's voting shares. In June 2008, the Storting approved an increase in the limit to 10 percent.[44] As of 30 September

---

43   "Government Pension Fund–Global, Second Quarter 2008," (Oslo: Norges Bank Investment Management, 2008).

44   Initially, Ingve Slyndstad, the fund's chief, had asked the government to allow up to 15 percent investment in individual companies. But the Storting agreed on 10 percent limit, which includes the 5 percent planned investment in real estate. For more information

2008, however, the fund's largest ownership interests with voting power in an individual company were approximately 6 percent.[45]

Ethical Investor

Perhaps the most significant development in the history of the fund is the introduction of the Ethical Guidelines by the Ministry of Finance. This is of paramount importance as the Guidelines set limitations of non–economic nature on the investment decision making of the fund. The Guidelines were officially issued in December 2005 pursuant to the regulations pertaining to the management of GPF–Global, dated 19 November 2004. The tenet of the Ethical Guidelines is that GPF–Global should not invest in areas or instruments that bear the risk of the fund contributing to "unethical acts or omissions, such as violation of fundamental humanitarian principles, serious violation of human rights, gross corruption or severe environmental damages."[46]

In 2008, the government conducted an evaluation of the Ethical Guidelines. The object of this evaluation was to "maintain broad–based [domestic] political support for the guidelines as well as to gather any feedback that may contribute to strengthening the profile of the fund as a socially responsible investor."[47] As a part of this evaluation, in January 2008, the Ministry of Finance organized an international conference in Oslo under the rubric of "Investing for the Future." Participants, who included academic figures, financial institutions, NGOs, and corporations, discussed the challenges of incorporating social and environmental factors into investment calculations and decision making processes.

The Ministry of Finance also held a public hearing on 18 June 2008, during which issues such as the need for changes or adjustments to existing policy measures, exercise of ownership rights, and the exclusion of companies from the GPF–Global were discussed. The Ministry also raised the question of whether "a minor part of the fund should be earmarked for special investment purposes, for example, within environmental technology or in developing countries."[48] The idea of a separate environmental fund was, however, abandoned later.

In complying with the Ethical Guidelines, Norges Bank (as the manager of GPF–Global) has two basic measures at its disposal. First, Norges Bank can exercise its "ownership rights" to safeguard the GPF–Global's long–term financial interests. In doing so, Norges Bank follows its own internal guidelines by taking

---

see: John Acher and Wojciech Moskwa, "Norway Oil Fund Big Buyer of Stocks, Eyes New Deals," *Reuters*, 29 May 2008.).

45   "Government Pension Fund–Global, Third Quarter 2008."

46   "The Ethical Guidelines," Ministry of Finance, Government of Norway, http://www.regjeringen.no/en.

47   "Chapter 5: The Management of the Government Pension Fund," 11.

48   Ibid.

into account the United Nations' Global Compact[49] and the OECD Guidelines for Corporate Governance[50] and Guidelines for Multinational Enterprises.[51] In 2008 Norges Bank held shares in about 7,000 companies around the world, participated in 6,857 general meetings, and voted in 6,143 of the meetings.[52] By 2010, the number of companies in which the fund held shares increased to 8,300 and Norges Bank continued to actively participate in annual general shareholder meetings.[53]

One interesting example of the exercise of ownership rights is the filing of a lawsuit in a Maryland Court in 2008 by GPF–Global, seeking to delay a meeting, previously scheduled for 23 December by Constellation shareholders, to vote for the takeover of their company by MidAmerican Energy Company, a unit of Warren Buffett's Berkshire Hathaway Incorporated.[54] GPF–Global held 4.8 percent shares in Constellation at the time. The GPF–Global's head of corporate governance, Anne Kvam, stated: "In our opinion, the MidAmerican agreement undervalues Constellation, and we expect the board to work for a solution that offers the highest value ... We are one of the biggest shareholders and take these necessary steps in order to safeguard our financial interests."[55] As a result of this involvement, MidAmerican Energy failed in its three–month long pursuit of Constellation on 17 December, when Constellation agreed to sell half of its business to the French energy giant Électricité de France.[56] A summary of Norges Bank activities with regard to voting at general meetings as well as its dialogues with large energy

---

49　The UN Global Compact is a strategic policy initiative for businesses that are committed to aligning their operations and strategies with ten universally accepted principles in the areas of human rights, labor, environment and anti–corruption.

50　The OECD principles for corporate governance are intended to assist both OECD and non–OECD governments to evaluate and improve the legal, institutional and regulatory framework for corporate governance in their countries, and to provide guidance and suggestions for stock exchanges, investors, corporations, and other parties.

51　The OECD Guidelines for Multinationals are a set of voluntary recommendations to multinational enterprises in major business ethics areas, including employment and industrial relations, human rights, environment, information disclosure, combating bribery, consumer interests, science and technology, competition, and taxation. For more information see http://www.oecd.org/department/0,3355,en_2649_34889_1_1_1_1_1,00.html.

52　"Government Pension Fund–Global, Second Quarter 2008."

53　"Government Pension Fund–Global, First Quarter 2010," 11.

54　MidAmerican offered $4.7 billion to take over the Constellation in September 2008. This move was backed by the Constellation's board. However, in December 2008, Électricité de France said it would offer $4.5 billion for half of the Constellation's nuclear assets and would give the company the option to sell up to $2 billion more of its nuclear assets.

55　Wojciech Moskwa, "Norway SWF Seeks to Block Buffett on Constellation," *Reuters*, 17 December 2008.

56　Colin Barr, "Constellation Loss a Win for Buffett," *CNNMoney.com*, 17 December 2008.

and multinational companies on various issues, including the climate change, environment, and child labor is published in the quarterly report.

The Norges Bank's second measure in complying with the Ethical Guidelines is the "negative screening and exclusion" of certain companies from the fund's investment universe. This task is accomplished through the Council on Ethics. The Council was established on 19 December 2004 with the purpose of providing evaluations of various investment opportunities and determining whether they are consistent with the fund's ethical principles. The Council currently consists of four highly–educated members with backgrounds in environmental science, law, economics, and human rights, and collects information independently and at its own discretion.[57] In addition to an annual activities report, the Council makes recommendations to the Ministry of Finance who in turn make decisions regarding the negative screening or exclusion of companies from the universe of possible investments. Upon a request from the Ministry, the Council also investigates whether an investment may violate Norway's obligations under international laws.

As early as 2004 and before the creation of the Council of Ethics, GPF–Global became indirectly involved in a power play involving foreign states and ethical issues. At the time, approximately 337 million krone of the GPF–Global (which was still referred to as the Oljefondet) was invested in stocks and bonds of Kerr–McGee Corporation. The company, through one of its subsidiaries (Kerr–McGee du Maroc Ltd.) had entered into an agreement with the state–owned Moroccan oil company (ONAREP) for oil exploration on the continental shelf, offshore Western Sahara. The area was a Moroccan–occupied territory, a situation that had made it the object of UN condemnations.[58]

In December 2004 the exile government of the Saharawi Arab Democratic Republic (SADR) and the Western Sahara Support Committee requested the Norwegian Ministry of Finance to exclude Kerr–McGee Corporation from GPF–Global's investment portfolio, on the grounds that Kerr–McGee, through its exploration activities, could enable Morocco to exploit the petroleum resources of the area. The Council regarded this as a serious violation of fundamental ethical norms, since it could strengthen Morocco's sovereignty claims and thereby contribute to the undermining of the UN peace process.[59] The company was excluded from the portfolio in 2005, a decision that was revoked only after a

57   The council initially had five members. For details on current members and their detailed background see: http://www.regjeringen.no/en/sub/Styrer–rad–utvalg/ethics_council/Councils–Activities/Council–Members.html?id=434895.

58   "Press Release 38/2005: Company Excluded from the Government Petroleum Fund," (Ministry of Finance, Norway, 2005).

59   Ibid.

review in 2006 and the suspension of the Kerr–McGee operations in the disputed areas.[60]

Negative screening of companies also includes those that either "produce weapons that through their normal use violate fundamental humanitarian principles; or sell weapons or military material to states mentioned in Clause 3.2 of the supplementary guidelines[61] for the management of the fund."[62] Additionally, companies whose activities create an unacceptable risk for the fund by contributing to any or a combination of the following items are excluded from the fund's investment universe:[63]

- serious or systematic human rights violations, such as murder, torture, deprivation of liberty, forced labor, the worst forms of child labor and other forms of child exploitation
- serious violation of individuals' rights in situations of war or conflict
- severe environmental damages
- gross corruption
- other particularly serious violations of fundamental ethical norms

Once a company is excluded from the investment universe, it will remain so until a regular review of excluded companies by the Council on Ethics establishes that the grounds for exclusion no longer exist. The Council will use the new information and recommend that the Ministry of Finance revoke the decision. The decision is then communicated to Norges Bank immediately. Norges Bank, on request from the Ministry of Finance, may convey to the companies the reason for the Ministry's decision.

Negative screening and compliance with the Ethical Guidelines in general is taken very seriously by government officials. In an interview, Finance Minister Halvorsen stated that while Norway would prefer not to exclude companies, it would not shirk its responsibility to exclude companies that commit violations of ethical precepts, such as human rights abuses, environmental pollution, and corruption.[64] The Ministry of Finance is also of the opinion that the negative screening should include both the producers and sellers of weapons and military matériel. For instance, the Ethical Guidelines ban investment in companies that sell weapons to Burma, in order to "prevent contributing to human rights violations as

---

60   "Press Release 62/2006: KerrMcGee Corporation Is Again Included in the Government Pension Fund–Global," (Ministry of Finance, Norway, 2006).

61   Surprisingly, Clause 3.2 of the Supplementary Guidelines for the management of the fund is exempt from disclosure. Source: Author's correspondence with the Norges Bank Investment Management, 31 August 2009.

62   "The Ethical Guidelines."

63   Ibid.

64   "Interview Norway's Halvorsen: Oil Fund to Grow in Tandem with Ethical Footprint," *Forbes*, 13 April 2007.

the result of the Burmese regime's systematic repression of its own population ...
Such a formulation of the new measure is also well aligned with, for example, US
and UK prohibition on the export of weapons and military material to Burma."[65]
In 2008, Clause 4.4 of the Ethical Guidelines was revised to include companies
that:

- Produce weapons that through their normal use violate fundamental
  humanitarian principles; or
- Sell weapons or military material to states mentioned in Clause 3.2. of the
  supplementary guidelines for the management of the fund.

In 2009, the Ministry of Finance excluded five companies from the fund's
portfolio on ethical grounds. Barrick Gold (Canada), the world's largest gold
mining company, was excluded from the fund's portfolio in January 2009. The
GPF–Global held shares in the company, valued at 1.25 billion krone at the end of
July 2008. The decision was made on the grounds of environmental damage.[66]

On 13 March 2009, the Ministry of Finance excluded Dongfeng Motor Group,
a Chinese company, from the GPF–Global investment universe. The company had
been under close observation since 2008 for its sale of trucks to Burma. The council
report indicated that the trucks were produced for or adapted to military purposes
and were therefore considered military equipment. Finance Minister Halvorsen
stated: "We cannot finance companies that support the military dictatorship in
Burma through the sale of military materials."[67]

Other companies GPF–Global divested from in 2009 included Textron
(US) for involvement in production of cluster weapons, Elbit Systems (Israel)
for production of surveillance systems, and Norilsk Nickel (Russia) for causing
environmental damage. Earlier, in December 2008, Norway hosted a conference
that agreed on a new international ban on cluster munitions. As a result, Textron
(US), in which GPF–Global held shares valued at 249 million krone at the end of
July 2008, was excluded due to the production of cluster munitions. The Finance
Minister Halvorsen, confirmed that "[t]he company produces cluster weapons,
which are banned pursuant to the Convention on Cluster Munitions."[68]

The Ministry of Finance has also asked the Council on Ethics to review the
companies, in which GPF–Global holds shares, that operate in the Palestinian
territories. At the end of 2007, the fund owned equities in 12 Israeli companies
and the bonds of three Israeli issuers. In early January 2009, after the Israel's
attack on the Gaza Strip, Finance Minister Halvorsen asked the Council on Ethics
to investigate whether the actions by companies in which the fund holds securities

---

65   "Chapter 5: The Management of the Government Pension Fund," 16.

66   "Norway Oil Fund Expels Two Companies," *Reuters*, 30 January 2009.

67   Marianne Stigset, "Norway Bans Dongfeng from Oil Fund; Siemens on Watch,"
Bloomberg, 13 March 2009.

68   "Norway Oil Fund Expels Two Companies."

and which operate in the Palestinian territories are in compliance with the Ethical Guidelines. The finance minster stressed:

> In the light of increased conflict level in the Palestinian areas, I will ask the Council on Ethics for an account of council's work on matters related to companies that have operations in these areas ... Investment in companies that contribute to an occupation against international law or oppression in occupied areas could be affected by both of these considerations [human rights abuses and violation of individuals' rights].[69]

Gro Nystuen, Head of the Council on Ethics, also reported that the Council had already begun re–reviewing the fund's investment in bonds issued by the state–owned Israel Electric Corporation (IEC), which supplies electricity to the Gaza Strip. He added, "[w]e are looking at all companies that might have activities in violation of the ethical guidelines, regardless of whether they are Israeli or operating in Israel."[70] The IEC went under the Council's review as early as April 2008, when it allegedly restricted power supply to the Gaza Strip. At the time, the Council on Ethics could not recommend excluding the IEC on the ground of a limited reduction in supply.[71]

Germany's Siemens AG, in which GPF–Global held shares valued at 6.3 billion krone (1.34 percent of the voting shares) as of December 2008, was also put under observation for four years on grounds of gross and systematic corruption. According to Finance Minister Halvorsen, in the event that new cases of gross corruption were uncovered, the company would be excluded from the fund's portfolio.[72]

Norwegian officials have continually publicly endorsed the adherence to the Ethical Guidelines. In June 2008, during a public hearing and seminar organized by the Ministry of Finance, issues including the exercise of ownership rights and exclusion of companies from the GPF–Global were discussed. There Finance Minister Halverson indicated that although banning an entire state is unlikely, she was open to discussing the matter during the ongoing review of the fund's Ethical Guidelines.[73] The GPF–Global has also black listed big names, many of them American Companies. Some of the excluded companied include Rio Tinto, Vedanta, Wal–Mart, BAE, Boeing, Honeywell, Northrop Grumman, EDS, Raytheon, GE Dynamics, L3 Communications, Lockheed Martin, and Thales.

---

69   Ibid.

70   John Acher, "Norway Oil Fund's Israel Holdings under Scrutiny," *Reuters*, 6 January 2009.

71   Ibid.

72   Stigset, "Norway Bans Dongfeng from Oil Fund; Siemens on Watch."

73   Aasa Christine Stoltz, "Norway Says Oil Fund Reluctant to Blacklist States," *Reuters*, 18 June 2008.

The realm of the Norwegian socially–responsible investment has also involved issues such as the global environment, health, and child labor. In 2010, the fund excluded 17 tobacco companies from its portfolio.[74] Norges Bank has continuously engaged with companies regarding their lobbying on legislation related to climate change. In June 2008, the United States Senate considered a major bill on the regulation of greenhouse gases. Although the bill did not come up for preliminary debate, Norges Bank held meetings with senior executives or high–level officers at six companies and aggressively pursued its environmental concerns during the second quarter of 2008.[75] In June 2009, Norges Bank officially added the climate change, water management, and children's rights to its ethical agenda.[76]

Norges Bank also arranged a meeting in India to engage multinational companies, active in cotton and vegetable seed production, in order to develop industry standards with regard to child labor. Norges Bank plans to develop standards for monitoring and reporting child labor in the region.[77] On 12 June 2009—the Word Day against Child Labor—four companies[78] in which GPF– Global holds equities announced that they will collaborate to fight against the use of child labor in seed production.[79]

Benign Economic Statecraft

Over the past 60 years, Norway has been a strong and durable parliamentary democracy with a constitutional monarchy, governed by a prime minister and a cabinet selected by the Storting (the Parliament). Norway has a long tradition of political participation by the public, along with respect for civil liberties and political rights. With a GDP of $276.3 billion, population of 4.8 million and a per capita income of $59.5 thousand in 2008, Norway is one of the richest countries in the world. As discussed earlier in this chapter, the Oljefondet (later GPF–Global) was established for the purpose of preserving the non–renewable energy resources, absorbing external financial shocks, and providing resources for the payment of

---

74   The excluded tobacco companies include, Alliance One International Inc., Altria Group Inc., British American Tobacco BHD, British American Tobacco Plc., Gudang Garam tbk pt., Imperial Tobacco Group Plc., ITC Ltd., Japan Tobacco Inc., KT&G Corp, Lorillard Inc., Philip Morris International Inc., Philip Morris Cr AS., Reynolds American Inc., Souza Cruz SA, Swedish Match AB, Universal Corp VA, and Vector Group Ltd.

75   "Government Pension Fund–Global, Second Quarter 2008."

76   "Government Pension Fund–Global, Second Quarter 2009."

77   "Government Pension Fund–Global, Second Quarter 2008."

78   These four companies included Monsanto (an international agriculture company), Syngenta (established after the merger between Novartis and AstraZeneca in November 2000 and became the first international company focusing exclusively on agribusiness), Bayer, and DuPont.

79   "Government Pension Fund–Global, Second Quarter 2009."

the state's future obligations. As Daniel Gross, the columnist for Newsweek and Slate, puts it:

> Norway has pursued a classically Scandinavian solution. It has viewed oil
> revenues as a temporary, collectively owned windfall that, instead of spurring
> consumption today, can be used to insulate the country from the storms of the
> global economy and provide a thick, goose–down cushion for the distant day
> when the oil wells run dry.[80]

As shown earlier in this chapter, when faced with the global financial crisis and the risk of recession, the government resorted to using the resources of GPF–Global in order to expand its rescue package while avoiding large budgetary deficits. But many of the fund's decision and investment strategies cannot be explained by economic thesis. For instance, in order to explain why, despite being profitable, specific companies or industries have been excluded from the portfolio, we need to look beyond the pure economic argument.

In the context of economic statecraft and the pursuit of power, we need to look at the relationship between the fund's management and the government, type of investment, and any statements by political elites about the purpose of the fund. As discussed, the Ministry of Finance is regarded as the owner of GPF–Global. The owner defines the structure of the benchmark portfolio in accordance with the consensus in the Storting, and by doing so it determines the main purpose of the fund. The fund is then managed by the investment management arm of Norges Bank as well as a number of external managers. Norges Bank is obliged to follow the benchmark portfolio but it has a defined deviation range. External managers have been managing only 11 to 14 percent of the portfolio and their function has been limited to technical management of their mandates.

There is a direct and close relationship between the fund's management and the political apparatus. The GPF–Global's management is free to act only within the limits set by the government. The fund managers also do not seem to have any influence over how the Ministry of Finance builds the benchmark portfolio, nor do they have any say in decisions regarding the inclusion or exclusion of companies from the portfolio. The government (Ministry of Finance) has also been including issues such as ethical and socially–responsible investment, human rights and labor rights, and environmental protection in the agenda.

The fund management has been obliged to follow these guidelines. Sanctioning (divestment) of a number of companies in which the fund held equities is one example. The fund's management uses active ownership as a tool to influence the decision–making process within the companies in which the fund holds shares. In a sense, the Ministry of Finance uses the GPF–Global's investment as leverage over

---

80   Daniel Gross, "Avoiding the Oil Curse, What Norway Can Teach Iraq," *Slate*, 29 October 2004.

companies whose activities contradict the values of the Ministry or the Council on Ethics, and in a broader sense, the Norwegian foreign policy.

The fund's leverage was, however, used in limited occasions such as divestments from companies involved in Western Sahara oil, selling trucks to Burma, or restricting electricity to Gaza strip. Moreover, the Norwegian government claims that divestment from major companies, such as Wal–Mart, Boeing, or Honeywell, is in line with the universally–accepted and internationally–endorsed values mandated by international organizations such as the United Nations or the OECD. The fact is that GPF–Global has never acquired any stakes in sensitive or controversial areas such as defense, nor has it invested in commercially irrational areas. Clearly, while the Norwegian fund may pursue political goals, it was never shown to be threatening to the foreign policy of Western states. This is what I have called benign economic statecraft, or the use of limited economic power for signaling political preferences.

The Norwegian government clearly communicates, to companies or states, its preferences with respect to what it deems unethical or in contradiction to the Norwegian foreign policy. Yet, Norway does not even manipulate the operation of those companies through divestment. In all cases, the Ministry of Finance gave Norges Bank about two months to sell the assets and the decision to sell was made public only after the sale was complete in order not to affect the sale price of the stocks.

Additionally, the amount of shares held in each of these companies was very small so the divestment of shares, which was done gradually over a two–month period, would not have negative impact on the company's equity prices or on the stock market. For instance, the GPF–Global's equity holdings of Elbit Systems or Dongfeng were less than 0.3 percent at the end of 2008. The fund's holdings in Textron, Barrick Gold, and Rio Tinto were only about 0.3, 0.6, and 0.1 percent, respectively, at the end of 2007.[81]

Norwegian officials have, on various occasions, attempted to present the fund as simply a financial entity with a precautionary and fully transparent approach, with the goal of long–term profitability, and no hidden or political agenda. For instance, in early 2008, Finance Minister Halvorsen was quoted as saying that the fund was "clearly a financial investor and not a strategic investor."[82] When asked about the losses GPF–Global incurred as a result of its holding in Lehman Brothers, Halvorsen maintained: "When you are an actor in the world markets, as we are through the pension fund, you have to expect both losses and gains ... Even if we sometimes suffer short–term losses, we also go through long periods of growth. Since we are long–term investors, our investments pay off, they do not

81   *Government Pension Fund-Global Annual Report 2007*. (Norges Bank Investment Management,2008).

82   John Acher, "Norway Seeks to up Wealth Fund's Ownership Cap," *Reuters*, 4 April 2008.

lose value."[83] This statement indicates that GPF–Global is not a speculative fund with a short–term investment horizon that may expose the recipient company as well as the host state to market volatility.

Nevertheless, in March 2008, when Martin Skancke, Director General of the Asset Management Department of the Norwegian Ministry of Finance, appeared before the House of Representatives to talk about GPF–Global and investment in the United States, he stated:

> While individual shareholders may sell their holdings of individual assets or funds they do not find ethically acceptable, the citizens of Norway have to accept to be the ultimate owners of the companies that the fund invests in. To preserve the legitimacy of the fund, it is important that the ownership in the various companies is acceptable for most citizens. Hence, the fund avoids investments in companies whose practices constitute an unacceptable risk that the fund is or will be complicit in what is deemed as grossly unethical activities.[84]

In his statement, Skancke maintained that the fund will be managed according to democratic principles and in a way that most Norwegian citizens would have chosen to invest their money, meaning the selection of instruments (equities or bonds) within the portfolio would reflect the democratic values of Norway, and not necessary the profitability of an instrument. As we saw, the fund was shown to be politically selective with respect to its investment choices.

This view was confirmed later when the Finance Minister Halvorsen, on the sidelines of a seminar organized by the Ministry of Finance in June 2008, clearly stated that "there could not be a large gap between Norway's foreign policy and the policy of the fund."[85] She even added: "I would guess that the conclusion also in the next round will be that we cannot run a separate foreign policy for states through the pension fund…"[86] This clearly indicates that GPF–Global acts according to the Norwegian foreign policy agenda by including political considerations in its decision–making. Those considerations are, in fact, the reflections of the Norwegian national system of political economy and foreign policy preferences.

For the Norwegian government, however, getting involved in domestic economic affairs is not anything new. Norway is an old democratic and pacifist state, highly dependent on the global economy, and at the same time, a model of welfare capitalism, featuring a combination of free markets and government intervention. In fact, Norway has a long history of state intervention in the

---

83   "Norway's Oil Fund Loses 61 Million Euros on Lehman Brothers," *AFP*, 15 September 2008.

84   The Committee on Financial Services, United States House of Representatives, *Statement by Director General Martin Skancke, Asset Management Department, Norwegian Ministry of Finance*, 5 March 2008.

85   Stoltz, "Norway Says Oil Fund Reluctant to Blacklist States."

86   Ibid.

domestic economy. Traditionally, the Norwegian government regulated the domestic economy heavily. Despite international waves of liberalization and privatization, the interest rate—an important monetary policy tool—was still set by the Storting until the 1980s. "The level of interest rates was an important part of the political game for power, and thus, they were set significantly below the market level."[87] Market intervention and control were not limited to the setting of interest rates and included many other areas. Even today, the Norwegian public sector is directly involved in the domestic economy, largely through state–owned enterprises (SOEs), in various organizational forms, in areas such as oil and gas, railroad passenger transportation, airline and civil aviation, power generation and distribution, and telecommunication.

In Norway, state has historically acted as an entrepreneur. State entrepreneurship takes several forms, including portfolio investment or capital investment and direct ownership (full or partial) of limited companies. According to an OECD report, "[a]bout three quarters of all Norwegian savings are controlled by the State, and state ownership in commercial entities is extensive both at the central and municipal level ... As an illustration, the State's holdings amount to about 40 per cent of the total value of the companies listed on the Oslo Stock Exchange."[88] This reflects both the history of Norway's industrial development and the significant role played by the state.

The state entrepreneurial thesis has also merits in the case of the GPF–Global. With extensive experience in managing the economy, the Norwegian government employs the fund in order to manage the national wealth. In doing so, the fund's management has delegated the management of the main portion of the fund to professionals within Norges Bank, and a small portion of the portfolio to external managers.

Additionally, GPF–Global has incessantly invested in riskier assets, with the view of higher returns. As discussed earlier, the share of the equities in the portfolio was increased from 40 percent in 2007 to more than 62 percent in 2010, suggesting a higher degree of risk taking by the government. This shows that the fund is not being used as a saving or purely precautionary deposit. If that were the case, the major part of the portfolio would have been invested in low–risk–low–return bonds. Therefore, in certain respects, the fund behavior can be explained by the state entrepreneurship thesis.

Finally, Norway's fund has also a number of characteristics that are consistent with the domestic compensatory purpose. Norway is a small and inherently open state. It has no influence over the terms of trade at which it is trading with the world and is therefore vulnerable to fluctuations in global commodity or financial markets. The contemporary industrial development history of Norway does not include any period of protectionism. Liberalism has been a main characteristic of

---

87   Grytten, "The Economic History of Norway."

88   OECD, "Regulatory Reform in Norway, Marketization of Government Services, State–Owned Enterprises," (2003).

both the Norwegian economy and society. Moreover, Norway is well aware of the limited life of its non–renewable energy resources and the burden of large public pension obligation in the near future. Despite that, GPF–Global has no current pension obligations and seems unlikely to have any in the near future.

Norway has been certainly exposed to financial hardship or external economic shocks. It has experienced the negative impact of reliance on the petroleum sector in the form of lower productivity, increasing wages, and subsequently loss of international competitiveness during the 1980s and 1990s. More recently, the country was impacted by the global financial meld down. In the wake of the recent global financial crisis, the Norwegian government transferred funds from GPF–Global to the budget to finance the stimulus package. Nevertheless, the action was more a temporary relief and did not reflect a long term reliance on the fund for budgetary purpose. The need for domestic compensation may be of indefinite duration, but the Norwegian government has not used GPF–Global as a regular source of funding. Instead, the Ministry of Finance has relied on the extensive tax system, with one of the highest rates in the world, as well as on financial discipline.

In summary, although the performance of GPF–Global, at first glance, seems consistent with all theoretical perspectives discussed earlier (economic statecraft, entrepreneurship, and domestic compensation), its operations, however, reflect the state's entrepreneurial competence in line with the Norwegian foreign policy agenda. The fund's commercial performance is constrained by a set of non–economic guidelines that are expressions of the national political consensus. GPF–Global is a tool for pursuing multiple goals including profitability and socially–responsible investment, with a focus on state's foreign policy agenda, encapsulated in Ethical Guidelines.

References

Acher, John. "Norway Oil Fund's Israel Holdings under Scrutiny." *Reuters*, 6 January 2009.

————. "Norway Seeks to up Wealth Fund's Ownership Cap." *Reuters*, 4 April 2008.

Acher, John, and Wojciech Moskwa. "Norway Oil Fund Big Buyer of Stocks, Eyes New Deals." *Reuters*, 29 May 2008.

"Background Note: Norway's Position in Relation to the International Debate on Sovereign Wealth Funds." Asset Management Department, The Norwegian Ministry of Finance, 2007.

Barr, Colin. "Constellation Loss a Win for Buffett." *CNNMoney.com*, 17 December 2008.

Berglund, Nina. "Oil Fund Takes 'Minor' Hit from U.S. Mortgage Crisis." *Aftenposten*, 26 August 2008.

"Chapter 2: Regulations on Management of the Government Pension Fund–Global." In *Provisions on the Management of the Government Pension Fund*: Ministry of Finance, Government of Norway.

"Chapter 5: The Management of the Government Pension Fund." In *National Budget 2009*: Ministry of Finance, Government of Norway.

Cowley, Elizabeth. "Oil–Rich Norway Sets Stimulus Plan " *Wall Street Journal Europe*, 27 January 2009.

"The Ethical Guidelines." Ministry of Finance, Government of Norway, http://www.regjeringen.no/en.

"External Trade in Commodities." Statistics Norway, http://www.ssb.no.

"FTSE." http://www.ftse.com/index.jsp.

Government Pension Fund-Global Annual Report 2007. Norges Bank Investment Management, 2008.

"Government Pension Fund–Global." Norges Bank, http://www.norges-bank.no/.

"Government Pension Fund–Global, First Quarter 2010." Oslo: Norges Bank Investment Management, 2010.

"Government Pension Fund–Global, Second Quarter 2008." Oslo: Norges Bank Investment Management, 2008.

"Government Pension Fund–Global, Second Quarter 2009." Oslo: Norges Bank Investment Management 2009.

"Government Pension Fund–Global, Third Quarter 2008." Oslo: Norges Bank Investment Management 2008.

Gross, Daniel. "Avoiding the Oil Curse, What Norway Can Teach Iraq." *Slate*, 29 October 2004.

Grytten, Ola. "The Economic History of Norway." In *EH.Net Encyclopedia*, edited by Robert Whaples, 2008.

International Monetary Fund. "IFS CD-ROM." Washington, D.C.: IMF, 2009.

"Interview Norway's Halvorsen: Oil Fund to Grow in Tandem with Ethical Footprint." *Forbes*, 13 April 2007.

Moskwa, Wojciech. "Norway SWF Seeks to Block Buffett on Constellation." *Reuters*, 17 December 2008.

Moskwa, Wojciech, and Camilla Knudsen. "Norway's Wealth Fund Says Was Prepared for Lehman." *Reuters*, 15 September 2008.

"Norway Enters Recession: Offical Data." *Agence France Presse*, 19 May 2009.

"Norway Oil Fund Expels Two Companies." *Reuters*, 30 January 2009.

"Norway SWF Takes Domestic View." *Thomson Merger News*, 31 December 2008.

"Norway to Dip into Oil Fund Due to Financial Crisis." *Agence France Presse*, 7 January 2009.

"Norway's Oil Fund Faces Losses in 2008." *Reuters*, 10 November 2008.

"Norway's Oil Fund Loses 61 Million Euros on Lehman Brothers." *AFP*, 15 September 2008.

"The Norwegian Oil History." Norwegian Petroleum Directorate (Oljedirektoratet), http://www.npd.no/English/Om+OD/Nyttig/Olje-ABC/Norsk+oljehistorie/70_tallet.htm.

OECD. "Regulatory Reform in Norway, Marketization of Government Services, State–Owned Enterprises." 2003.

"OLF the Norwegian Oil Industry Association." http://www.olf.no/about-olf/category292.html.

"Press Release 38/2005: Company Excluded from the Government Petroleum Fund." Ministry of Finance, Norway, 2005.

"Press Release 48/2009: Revised National Budget 2009: Continued Expansionary Policies." Ministry of Finance, Norway, 2009.

"Press Release 62/2006: KerrMcGee Corporation Is Again Included in the Government Pension Fund–Global." Ministry of Finance, Norway, 2006.

"Provisions on the Management of the Government Pension Fund." Ministry of Finance, Government of Norway.

The Committee on Financial Services, United States House of Representatives. *Statement by Director General Martin Skancke, Asset Management Department, Norwegian Ministry of Finance*, 5 March 2008.

Stigset, Marianne. "Norway Bans Dongfeng from Oil Fund; Siemens on Watch." *Bloomberg*, 13 March 2009.

———. "Shell Gas Find in Norway May Be Biggest in 12 Years." *Bloomberg*, 19 June 2009.

Stoltz, Aasa Christine. "Norway Says Oil Fund Reluctant to Blacklist States." *Reuters*, 18 June 2008.

"The World Fact Book." CIA, https://www.cia.gov/library/publications/the-world-factbook/docs/rankorderguide.html.

Chapter 4
How Abu Dhabi Investment Authority Became an Entrepreneur

This chapter presents the second case study of SWFs, the Abu Dhabi Investment Authority (ADIA) of the United Arab Emirates. Although ADIA has been in existence since the mid–1970s, only in the past few years has the fund appeared in the headlines. The exact size of the fund is still debated. Many analysts and market observers believe that the fund is the world largest SWF, with an estimated value of between $400 billion and $875 billion[1], and sometimes even more. Some others, however, estimate the size of the assets under ADIA's management, in the wake of the global financial crisis, to be below $300 billion, making ADIA the second largest fund after GPF–Global of Norway.

Despite lack of official information about the size of the fund, there is evidence suggesting that the fund's performance is more in line with the state entrepreneurship and domestic compensation perspectives than the economic statecraft thesis. State entrepreneurship provides a relevant context for the study of ADIA's modest management, while domestic compensation argument offers some additional insights to the formation and purpose of the fund. Although the United Arab Emirates enjoyed an overall balance of payment surplus, the country has relied on ADIA as a source of financing for the budget on various occasions. ADIA is also considered as one of the least transparent funds, although this has changed to some extent in recent years. The opacity of the fund, however, does not necessarily reflect deliberate secrecy or political agenda. It can be a cultural issue or it may be due to the lack of developed organizational procedures or standards similar to those in well–established western financial entities.

Although ADIA is technically a sub–national fund, it qualifies as a sovereign fund for several reasons. First, ADIA is the largest fund of Abu Dhabi, which is the driving force of the Emirates both economically and politically. Abu Dhabi is endowed with most of the United Arab Emirates' natural resources and is the federation's fiscal "heavyweight". Second, ADIA is also the Emirate's largest fund and the Emirates' president is chairman of the board of directors. And third, ADIA is involved in large investments in many different areas, both geographically and industry–wise. Since 2008, the fund has shifted its focus solely on markets outside of its region.

In this chapter, I will discuss the politico–economic circumstances that existed prior to the establishment of the fund and the domestic political dynamics that led

---

1   Andrew England, "ADIA Makes Play for a Native Minority," *Financial Times*, 16 November 2008.

to the decision to establish the fund. As will be discussed, although many political processes in the United Arab Emirates still remain traditional, ADIA has strived to modernize its management structure and decision making processes, and to build up a well diversified portfolio. An examination of the way in which ADIA's assets were used or where they were invested in during the periods of economic prosperity provides us with insight into the underlying motives of the fund.

Despite its long history, ADIA remains one of the least–transparent sovereign funds, even after recent efforts to promote ADIA's public image. The members of the board of directors of the fund—who were previously barred from speaking to the media and public about the fund—held interviews on limited occasions. ADIA also hired public relations professionals and made some information about its portfolio available on its website. Despite the changes, still, many details about the fund such as the size of its holdings, audit reports, or financial statements remain unavailable to the public.

A Good Idea at the Right Time

The history of ADIA dates back to the creation of the federation of seven former Trucial States in December 1971, known today as the United Arab Emirates.[2] Oil exploration in the region started in the 1930s and was pursued vigorously after World War II in various parts of the then Trucial States. Oil was discovered for the first time off–shore Abu Dhabi in August 1958 and in 1962 exportation began from Das Island. One year later an on–shore field was discovered in Abu Dhabi and vast revenues began to pour into the emirate. However, Sheikh Shakhbut bin Sultan Al Nahyan, Amir of Abu Dhabi at the time, refused to allow the oil money to be spent because "[w]hat he feared most was the disintegration of the social fabric of Abu Dhabi in the face of such an extraordinary windfall ... he honestly believed that maintenance of the status quo was the only way to save Abu Dhabi."[3]

Sheikh Shakhbut's resistance to change and development was one of the main reasons that made the rest of the Al Nahyan family—who believed that change was both vital and inevitable—encourage him to step down. Sheikh Shakhbut was replaced by his younger brother, Sheikh Zayed bin Sultan Al Nahyan, who brought a great deal of experience and knowledge about administration to the office. In November 1971, just before the creation of the United Arab Emirates, the Abu Dhabi National Oil Company (ADNOC) was established. Since then, the Emirate's

---

2   The United Arab Emirates is a federation of seven former Trucial States, i.e., Abu Dhabi, Dubai, Sharjah, Ras–Al–Khaimah, Ajman, Umm al–Qaiwain, and Fujairah. Trucial States refer to the states (Sheikhdoms), whose rulers had signed the Perpetual Maritime Truce with the British government in 1853, which called to end all hostilities at sea.

3   Rosemarie Said Zahlan, *The Making of the Modern Gulf States: Kuwait, Bahrain, Qatar, the United Arab Emirates, and Oman*, Rev. and updated ed. (Reading, Berkshire, U.K.: Ithaca Press, 1998), 110.

oil affairs have been conducted mainly through this state enterprise, although after the creation of United Arab Emirates, the new constitution stipulated that the rulers of the individual emirates retain control over their respective oil resources.[4]

Sheikh Zayed, Amir of Abu Dhabi—who became the first president of the United Arab Emirates in December 1971—strived to ensure the prosperity and development of the federation to the extent that he dissolved the Abu Dhabi cabinet in 1973, then merged it with that of the United Arab Emirates, and offered Abu Dhabi's oil revenues to finance developmental projects in the federation.[5] Abu Dhabi was the richest of the seven emirates in petroleum resources to the extent that "[b]y 2000, Abu Dhabi controlled 90 percent of the country's oil and more than 85 percent of its gas reserves."[6]

In 1976, Sheikh Zayed established ADIA. The sole source of ADIA's revenue, since then, has been the profits from the petroleum sector. The ADNOC transfers its net profit—which may vary year by year depending on both oil prices and the volume of exports—to the Abu Dhabi Department of Finance. Subsequently, the Abu Dhabi Department of Finance allocates one part of ADNOC's net profits to ADIA and the other part to the emirate's budget.[7]

Although detailed information on the early stages of the fund is not available— a situation consistent with the relative unavailability of other official data for the United Arab Emirates—there is little doubt that ADIA has played a significant role in maintaining the economic prosperity of both the emirate of Abu Dhabi and the United Arab Emirates, especially at times of economic contraction.

In order to examine the role ADIA played in alleviating the Emirates' economic problems, we need to first look at the relationship between the oil sector, the budget, and ADIA. The central place of the petroleum sector in the United Arab Emirates' economy is evident. The volatility in oil markets has a direct impact on both the overall (federal) budget and the individual emirates' budgets. In the United Arab Emirates, "the individual emirates tend to exercise great autonomy over spending plans, and emirates have their own budgets."[8] In fact the rulers of each emirate retain control over their oil and gas resources by provisions of the Constitution. For both the federal and Abu Dhabi budgets, the revenue from the oil sector is the main source of income. Table 4.1 shows the level of budget reliance on the oil and gas sector. As can be seen, since the turn of the century, more than 65 percent of the federal budget was financed through the oil and gas sector. The corresponding figure for the Abu Dhabi budget was more than 75 percent.

---

4   Malcolm C. Peck, *The United Arab Emirates: A Venture in Unity*, Profiles. Nations of the Contemporary Middle East. (Boulder, Colo.: Westview Press, 1986).

5   Zahlan, *The Making of the Modern Gulf States: Kuwait, Bahrain, Qatar, the United Arab Emirates, and Oman*.

6   Andrea B. Rugh, *The Political Culture of Leadership in the United Arab Emirates* (New York: Palgrave Macmillan, 2007), 8.

7   It is not clear what or who determines the allocation.

8   Peck, *The United Arab Emirates: A Venture in Unity*, 116.

Table 4.1   Federal government finances and Abu Dhabi fiscal operations (Dh billion)

	Federal government total revenue	of which from oil & gas sector	Share of oil & gas sector of total revenue	Abu Dhabi fiscal revenue	of which from oil & gas sector	Share of oil & gas sector of total revenue
1991	61.8	38.7	63%	52.2	32.3	62%
1992	56.2	37.2	66%	42.0	29.4	70%
1993	48.8	32.0	66%	36.7	24.5	67%
1994	50.0	28.7	57%	38.1	22.7	60%
1995	57.4	32.0	56%	44.2	25.5	58%
1996	65.1	37.0	57%	49.8	30.7	62%
1997	70.5	41.1	58%	53.3	34.3	64%
1998	61.4	25.5	42%	44.6	21.4	48%
1999	54.7	30.1	55%	37.1	25.2	68%
2000	89.7	60.0	67%	69.5	52.6	76%
2001	78.4	51.6	66%	58.9	45.5	77%
2002	79.4	55.0	69%	46.0	36.4	79%
2003	100.0	75.5	76%	61.1	51.8	85%
2004	134.9	99.6	74%	85.6	68.0	79%
2005	203.7	152.8	75%	131.6	104.3	79%
2006	299.0	229.4	77%	194.4	157.1	81%
2007	333.4	234.5	70%	224.0	168.3	75%

Sources: IMF Country Reports 03/67 (years 1991–1998), IMF Country Report 04/174 (year 1999), IMF Country Report 06/256 (years 2000–2001), IMF Country Report 07/348 (year 2002), and IMF Country Report 09/120 (years 2003–2007).

The federal government depends largely on grants from Abu Dhabi and Dubai for the funding of its budget. This reliance was substantial, especially prior to 2003, when the Emirates' budget experienced deficits as a result of loose fiscal policy and large government expenditures. The recent global financial crisis had also an adverse effect on the economy of the United Arab Emirates.

ADIA has played a smoothing role in the economy of the United Arab Emirates. The nature and significance of this role, however, is somewhat obscured by both general lack of information and the inconsistency of international statistics (both variables and observations). Table 4.2 shows the federal government's consolidated balance of budget as well as sources of financing during two periods for which consistent data was available.[9] Although the budget methodology has slightly changed over time—which might explain why data is inconsistent—even the inconsistent data show the same phenomenon, i.e., frequent (almost continuous) federal budget deficits until 2003, followed by five consecutive years of surplus.

Table 4.2   Consolidated federal budget (Dh billion)

	Overall balance	Bank financing	Non–bank financing *
1993	−15.0	−2.7	17.7
1994	−20.5	02.2	18.3
1995	−21.0	−3.0	24.0
1996	−25.2	02.1	23.1
1997	0–9.5	00.6	08.9
2003	08.4	0–2.3	0–6.1
2004	38.4	0–1.8	−36.6
2005	99.3	−16.0	−83.2
2006	171.3	0–4.6	−166.8
2007	166.4	0–9.5	−156.9

Sources: IMF Country Reports 09/120 (years 2003–2007) and IMF Country Report 98/134 (years 1993–1997)

* This item has taken different names in various reports. For the period 1993–1997, it was referred to as "exceptional financing"

The budget deficit has been financed through accounts that have taken different titles over time. These titles include resident or domestic banks, non–banks, official

---

9   The main source of data on the United Arab Emirates' economy is the IMF Country Reports. However, in some cases the same observation takes different values in various country reports. To correct for this, the latest available report containing the specific observation was used. Additionally, in some cases the definition of a given variable and its accounting methodology has changed from one report to the next. This makes the comparison of the data over time quite difficult. Where inconsistencies could not be explained, the data was excluded from the research.

foreign reserves, privatization receipts, and exceptional financing. ADIA has been specifically mentioned once as a source of financing for the budget deficit, in the 1998 IMF Country Report covering the period 1993–1997.[10] In that report, only two accounts were shown under the financing; one was "domestic banks" and the other "exceptional financing," a title that was never used again. The relevant footnote indicated that the exceptional financing included "use of investment income and transfers from ADIA's foreign assets."

Although ADIA has not been specifically mentioned in subsequent reports as a source of financing, it is reasonable to assume that between 1993 and 1997 the fund has been used to finance the federal government's expenditures. It is also possible that during the subsequent years of budget deficit, ADIA's resources (investment income or foreign assets) were used for the same purpose; especially considering the fact that the United Arab Emirates' budget has a low tax base and is highly dependent on the oil income.

At the individual emirate level, the investment income has been a significant part of the Abu Dhabi budget (see Table 4.3). Although there is no detailed information about the components of the investment income, it is very likely that the major part of the investment income in Abu Dhabi's budget was driven by ADIA's returns, considering ADIA as the Emirates' largest fund.[11] As shown in Table 4.3, the investment income included in the total revenue of Abu Dhabi's budget rose from about Dh 34 billion in 2006 to more than Dh 46 billion in 2007, and its share of the total revenues varied between about 12 percent and 26 percent between 1999 and 2007.

Most likely, ADIA has also played a major role in slowing down the impact of the recent financial crisis. In the wake of the global financial crisis, the Emirates Central Bank had to inject funds into the domestic banking sector to address the liquidity shortage. In fact, the Central Bank guaranteed the external liabilities of all Emirati banks. The Central Bank foreign assets, which grew sharply between 2003 and 2007, mainly due to high oil prices, shrunk by more than one–third to Dh 201.4 billion in March 2009.[12]

Despite the impact of the global financial crisis, some analysts in the region still believe that the external factors did not have a major impact on the management of assets of the United Arab Emirates, including those controlled by the wealth funds. For instance, according to an analyst at the National Bank of Kuwait, "[s]ignificant though these shifts have been, it is important to note that they do not equate to changes in the UAE's 'income.' Nor do they reflect any change in overall strategy

---

10   This is different from ADIA's return on investment that is likely a revenue item on the budget under the title "investment income."

11   Only in the 2009 IMF Country Report is there a reference to the "transfer of earnings of sovereign wealth funds" as a component of the "investment income" item. Most likely, the reference is made to ADIA.

12   Daniel Kaye, "UAE Money Data Reveals Financial System under Stress," (National Bank of Kuwait, 2009).

regarding the country's huge total stock of foreign assets, the bulk of which are managed not by the CBUAE [Central Bank of United Arab Emirates] but by the Abu Dhabi Investment Authority (ADIA)."[13] The decision to establish ADIA, made by Sheikh Zayed more than 40 years ago when the United Arab Emirates was enjoying windfall of oil revenues without corresponding expenditures, has proved to be prudent and still relevant today.

Table 4.3   Abu Dhabi fiscal operations and share of investment income (Dh billion)

	Total Revenue	Of which investment income *	Share of investment income of total revenue	Overall balance
1999	37.1	09.7	26.10%	−10.1
2000	69.5	15.1	21.70%	5.8
2001	59.0	11.6	19.70%	−17.4
2002	46.0	08.1	17.60%	−20.3
2003	61.1	07.2	11.80%	−8.8
2004	85.6	13.9	16.20%	13.4
2005	131.6	24.6	18.70%	51.7
2006	194.4	33.7	17.30%	120.1
2007	224.0	46.3	20.70%	102.2

Sources: IMF Country Reports 04/174 (year 1999), IMF Country Report 06/256 (years 2000–2001), IMF Country Report 07/348 (year 2002), and IMF Country Report 09/120 (years 2003–2007).

* IMF staff estimate

Learning Along the Way

During its early stages, ADIA was a relatively unsophisticated fund mainly due to a lack of local talent.[14] The administrative structure of the Emirati fund expanded gradually over years. Between 1988 and 1993 the number of fund employees doubled[15] and by 2010 surpassed one thousand. Today, about 60 percent of the employees come from outside the United Arab Emirates. Lack of local talent has always been an issue for the fund. In order to tackle this problem, ADIA announced

13   Ibid., 3.

14   Karen Remo-Listana, "Wealth Funds in the UAE Lead Way with Transparency," *Emirates Business 24|7*, 3 March 2009.

15   ADIA had about 500 employees in 1988. By 1993, this number jumped to over one thousand.

a new recruitment program[16] in 2008 to ensure that it has a ready pipeline of local talent.[17]

Especially since the turn of the century and the political scrutiny over the nature of SWFs, ADIA has hired veteran public relations and communication professionals to improve its image, especially in the West. In 2008, ADIA hired Burson–Marsteller, an American public relations company, and later appointed former Morgan Stanley communications specialists[18] as resident communications experts.[19] Concurrently with that, prominent western financial experts were hired to lead various departments in ADIA. These experts were veterans of major financial companies such as Morgan Stanley or Goldman Sachs.

Until recently, ADIA's senior officials were not even allowed to be interviewed by the media. In 2008, Sheikh Ahmed bin Zayed Al Nahyan, managing director of ADIA at the time, gave an exclusive interview to Business Week, revealing some details of the fund's portfolio, investment approach, and agenda. [20] Almost two years later, on 11 January 2010, he held another interview this time with the German daily Handelsblatt, where he disclosed little information about portfolio composition and its geographical distribution, while leaving the size of assets under the management of the fund undisclosed.

Another initiative taken by ADIA was the redesign of its website. In 2010, the simplistic website of ADIA—which contained very little useful information about the fund—was upgraded to include more public relations material and some financial content that was previously not available to the public. Additionally, ADIA's first annual report (ADIA Review 2009) was published, however, the report did not contain much more information than the website.

In practice, ADIA is run by a board of directors that has absolute control over all aspects of the fund's operations. The board of directors consists of ten members the majority of whom come from the influential family of Al Nahyan. The current Chairman of ADIA is Sheikh Khalifa bin Zayed Al Nahyan who is both the ruler of Abu Dhabi and the president of the United Arab Emirates. He was named president

---

16   ADIA selects students in their last year of high school and sponsors them through their graduation from university. The scheme attracted 400 high school applicants in the first year, but only 18 were accepted. The applicants are mostly sent to universities in the United States. Reportedly, ADIA spends about $10 million on training annually.

17   England, "ADIA Makes Play for a Native Minority."

18   Erik Portanger was appointed as the new head of media relations of ADIA. Prior to ADIA, he was responsible for corporate communications at Morgan Stanley in the United Kingdom. Also, earlier in May 2008, Euart Glendinning was appointed as the first global head of corporate communications and public affairs.

19   Remo-Listana, "Wealth Funds in the UAE Lead Way with Transparency."; Victoria Barbary and Edward Chin, "Testing Time, Sovereign Wealth Funds in the Middle East & North Africa and the Global Financial Crisis," (London: Monitor Company Group L.P., 2009).

20   Emily Thornton and Stanley Reed, "A Power Player Emerges in the Gulf," *BusinessWeek*, no. 4089 (2008).

by the Federal Council shortly after the death of his father, Sheikh Zayed bin Sultan Al Nahyan, the engineer of the Emirates' development plan, who died in November 2004. All other board members are appointed by the ruler's decree.

Until March 2010, Sheikh Ahmed bin Zayed Al Nahyan, the twelfth son of Sheikh Zayed bin Sultan, served as the managing director of the fund. He was a graduate of the University of Al–Ain in Abu Dhabi and joined ADIA as an equity analyst in 1992. He rejected the traditional investment philosophy of the fund that dated almost two decades earlier, when the fund was first conceived under the direction of a British colonial officer and a local advisor to the royal family and modeled after British pension funds. During Sheikh Ahmed's tenure, ADIA's management underwent a number of changes. In 1993, only a year after Sheikh Ahmed joined ADIA, the fund's executives decided to peg the fund's holdings to global economic growth.[21] In the same year, ADIA's management introduced benchmarks and started to formalize asset allocation procedures. ADIA kept the structure of the benchmark portfolio secret until 2009, when it published its first official annual review (see Table 4.4).

In 2007, ADIA's office moved to a new location and its management initiated further organizational realignment. ADIA has restructured its organizational structure a few times. In 2008, it merged various functional areas—including risk, compliance, and performance—and created the Investment Services Department with the aim of providing greater administrative, IT, and analytical support to investment departments. In March 2010, the managing director of ADIA died in a plane crash in Morocco. Subsequently, Sheikh Khalifa bin Zayed Al Nahyan, the chairman of the board and president of the United Arab Emirates, reshuffled the board and appointed Sheikh Hamed Bin Zayed Al Nahyan as the new managing director on 13 April 2010.[22]

In terms of investment, ADIA's strategy has also developed over time. At the beginning, the fund focused on investing in bonds, equities, and real estate in the country and in the region. In 1986, a decade after its inception, ADIA entered into the commodity business. Later in 1989, private equities were added to the portfolio. In 1993, ADIA's managers instituted strict guidelines to peg the fund's holdings to global economic growth. The decision quickly proved to be strategically critical. ADIA reduced its large positions in Japanese equities just before the Japanese stock market began a 15–year decline.[23] After almost a decade, in 1998, inflation–indexed bonds were introduced to ADIA's portfolio. In 2005, ADIA's focus shifted to the emerging markets and subsequently the Emerging Markets department was created. This shift indicated a change in the risk tolerance of the fund and that maximizing investment return was becoming a major objective.

---

21   Ibid.

22   "Khalifa Names New Managing Director for Adia," *Gulfnews.com*, 14 April 2010.

23   Thornton and Reed, "A Power Player Emerges in the Gulf."

Perhaps the most significant organizational change took place in late 2007 when it was decided that ADIA's local and regional portion of its investment portfolio be transferred to Abu Dhabi Investment Council (ADIC). Subsequently, ADIA divested its domestic assets for an undisclosed amount to ADIC in 2008.[24] Along with this change, the Abu Dhabi Investment Company (ADICo.),[25] which was established in 1977 and had acted as an executive arm of ADIA, was placed under the ADIC administration. Figure 4.1 presents a timeline of the evolution of the fund.

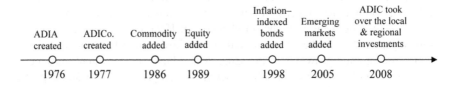

Figure 4.1   Timeline of the evolution of ADIA

However, as early as the summer of 2007, the fund was faced with a problem in its asset allocation. When the market plunged, the fund became underweighted in American stocks. One solution was a single–shot investment. In late November 2007, ADIA decided to buy up to 4.9 percent of Citigroup Inc. bonds at a total value of $7.5 billion with no special right of ownership or control and no role in the management or governance of Citigroup.[26] The units were convertible at a price of between $31.42 and $37.24 a share between 15 March 2010 and 15 September 2011, but the price of Citigroup shares did not recover—they fell even further. As early as 18 September 2008, shares of Citigroup closed at $16.65 per unit, resulting in a loss of $3.53 billion.[27] Since then, ADIA has attempted to control damages by a December 2009 filing of an arbitration claim against Citigroup on the basis of "fraudulent misrepresentations."[28]

As with many other funds, ADIA—which had a large portion of its portfolio in equities—was hit hard during the recent global financial crisis. Setser and Ziemba

---

24   Barbary and Chin, "Testing Time, Sovereign Wealth Funds in the Middle East & North Africa and the Global Financial Crisis."

25   ADICo. also offers treasury services, loan syndication, equity and debt underwriting as well as asset management and brokerage. It made the news when it reportedly was it talks to buy the Chrysler Building in New York City for about $800 million. (Source: Remo-Listana, "Wealth Funds in the UAE Lead Way with Transparency.")

26   "Citigroup to Sell 47.5 Billion in Equity Units to Abu Dhabi Investment Authority," *The Associated Press*, 27 November 2007.

27   Craig Karmin and Carolyn Cui, "Smart–Money Bets on Street Turn Sour-Big Investors Find Some Big Losses; 'Stakes on the Cheap'," *The Wall Street Journal*, 19 September 2008.

28   Dankin Campbell and Andrew MacAskill, "Abu Dhabi Fund Seeks to End Citigroup Share Purchase," *Bloomberg*, 16 December 2009.

estimated that the value of the assets under the management of ADIA and ADIC fell by $180 billion in 2008.[29] The Institute of International Finance was also quoted as having estimated the value of ADIA's assets in 2009 at about $282 billion, as a result of both the market crisis and speculative investment decisions.[30]

Since 2008, ADIA has been at the forefront of the development of the Santiago Principles[31] and an advocate of greater transparency. Hamed Al Hurr Al Suwaidi, Undersecretary of the Abu Dhabi Department of Finance and one of ADIA's directors, has been one of the active participants in the International Working Group of SWFs, chairing the forum leading to the Santiago Principles. He has been quoted as saying "[i]t's all about trust ... It's about collectively doing everything in our power to ensure that trust lies in the heart of everything we do."[32]

Prior to the development of the Santiago Principles, ADIA attempted to address the concerns about transparency by individually sending letters to a number of states and international institutions. ADIA sent a three–page letter—dated 12 March and signed by Abu Dhabi's director for international affairs, Yousef Al Otaiba—to the United States secretary of the treasury at the time, Henry Paulson, in order to clarify for the United States and Europe the intent of Abu Dhabi's government managed investment funds. The letter was also sent to the finance ministers of the other G7 states, the IMF, the World Bank, OECD, and the European Commission.[33] In the letter, principles such as "independent, commercially driven investment decisions" and adherence to "all laws, regulations, and rules of the countries its funds invest in," were stressed.

In an interview with IMF Survey online, Al Suwaidi maintained: "Now that the principles are a public document, non–implementation or non–compliance will become clear in a short period of time, especially as some of the principles call for certain information to be disclosed. In addition, we are considering the establishment of a permanent representative body for SWFs."[34] Despite all these efforts, ADIA remains closed to outside enquiries.[35] Even the L–M Transparency Index for ADIA did not change over the past few years and remained very low.[36]

---

29   Brad Setser and Rachel Ziemba, "GCC Sovereign Funds, Reversal of Fortune," (New York: Council on Foreign Relations, Center for Geoeconomic Studies, 2009).

30   Nadim Kawach, "UAE's Overseas Invetsmnet Income to Rebound in 2009," *Emirates Business 24|7*, 20 April 2009.

31   See f.n. 21 in Chapter 3 for more details.

32   Remo-Listana, "Wealth Funds in the UAE Lead Way with Transparency."

33   The letter was also published on the Wall Street Journal. See: Yousef Al–Otaiba, "Our Sovereign Wealth Plans," *The Wall Street Journal*, 10 March 2008.

34   "Wealth Funds' Long–Term View May Help Stablize Markets," *IMF Survey*, 16 October 2008.

35   After several attempts in contacting ADIA's media relations department, the first question I was asked was whether any of the information I had requested would be made public or not. Subsequent correspondences remained unanswered.

36   The L–M Transparency Index assigned by the SWF Institute remained was 'three' in January 2009.

Today, ADIA is thought to be one of the world's largest SWFs. The Saudi American Bank (SAMBA) has estimated the size of the portfolio under ADIA's management at the end of 2007 to be between $335 billion and $875 billion.[37] Media and business analysts' estimates of the size of the fund range from $500 billion to $900 billion.[38] However, in the aftermath of the global financial crisis, estimates of the size of the fund were revised drastically. In 2009, two researchers at the Council on Foreign Relations (CFR) attempted to estimate the size of the Emirati fund. Setser and Ziemba built a model using oil price data and relevant IMF data and concluded that the size of assets managed by ADIA had been overestimated, sometimes by as much as 100 percent. They estimated the total size of ADIA and ADIC as of December 2008 at $328 billion.[39] The Institute of International Finance also revised its estimate of the size of ADIA's assets from $372 billion at the end of 2007 to about $282 billion at the end of 2008,[40] which would make the fund second in size to the GPF–Global of Norway.

Despite its efforts, ADIA still remains one of the world's least transparent fund, with none of its financial reports (including the value of assets under its management) or information concerning its investment decision–making process available to the public. Some of ADIA's major investments will be discussed in the next section, but for now suffice to say that the fund's investment strategy and administrative structure has evolved over a period of more than three decades. The rate of change and transformation of ADIA's management and investment strategy has been somewhat sluggish, with processes that still remain traditional.

Expansion in All Directions

The investment choices of ADIA—in terms of geography, type of instrument, and industry sector—have expanded, especially over the past two decades. Today, a major portion of ADIA's portfolio is invested in various types of equities (up to 78 percent). Investment in sovereign bonds constitutes 10 to 20 percent of the portfolio. In terms of geographical distribution of the portfolio, ADIA's focus is on assets in North America and Europe. Table 4.4, which became public only recently, presents the structure of the benchmark portfolio. Many analysts had previously estimated the average annual return on ADIA's portfolio since 1976 at about 10 percent.[41] The official data revealed, however, that as of December

---

37   "The UAE Economy: Sustainable in the Face of a Serious Global Recession ", (Riadh: Samba Financial Group, 2009).

38   Christopher S. Rugaber, "Abu Dhabi Lays out Investment Principles for Its Government–Run Wealth Fund," *The Associated Press*, 18 March 2008.

39   Setser and Ziemba, "GCC Sovereign Funds, Reversal of Fortune."

40   Nadim Kawach, "Bond Issues to Help Boost UAE," *Emirates Business 24|7*, 3 May 2009.

41   Thornton and Reed, "A Power Player Emerges in the Gulf."

2009, the average annual returns over the past 30 and 20 years have been 8 percent and 6.5 percent respectively.[42] According to ADIA's first official report (ADIA Annual Review 2009), about 80 percent of the fund's assets are managed by external managers and about 60 percent of the assets are invested in indexed instruments.[43]

Table 4.4   ADIA's benchmark portfolio structure (percent)

By Asset Class	
Equities (developed countries)	35–45
Equities (emerging markets)	10–20
Small Cap equities	1–5
Private equity	2–8
Government bonds	10–20
Real estate	5–10
Infrastructure	1–5
Alternative investment *	5–10
Credit	5–10
Cash	0–10
By Region	
North America	35–50
Europe	25–35
Developed Asia	10–20
Emerging Markets	15–25

Source: "ADIA Review 2009"

* Includes investment in hedge funds and managed funds.

As discussed earlier, ADIA has come a long way in its efforts to more skillfully manage its assets. Although ADIA does not disclose information about its investments, some of its transactions, especially the recent and large ones, have made their way into the media. ADIA claims that it does not take controlling stakes in companies, usually acquiring less than 4.5 percent of a company.[44] Nevertheless, investment data published by the media sometimes show large holdings.

Since 2007, ADIA has focused on acquiring financial firms, banks, or brokerage houses. In 2007, ADIA acquired about an eight percent stake in the regional investment bank EFG–Hermes. The investment bank was established in Egypt in 1984 and its activities included brokerage, asset management, and investment banking. EFG–Hermes has established a presence in the markets of Gulf Cooperation Council (GCC) members, specifically the United Arab Emirates

---

42   "Khalifa Names New Managing Director for Adia," 3.
43   Ibid.
44   Remo-Listana, "Wealth Funds in the UAE Lead Way with Transparency."

in 2005 and Saudi Arabia in 2007. The position gave ADIA a seat on the EFG–Hermes Holdings Board of Directors.[45]

In the same year, ADIA in a competition against six other institutional players took about a 20 percent stake in the private equity firm Ares Management.[46] Ares became a hot commodity after its managing partner, Tony Ressler, revealed a plan to buy distressed debt. According to Ressler, ADIA was chosen as it "seemed to care" about long–term performance rather than short–term gains.[47] Other investments by ADIA included a 10 percent holding in Qatar Telecom, 0.07 percent in Ecopetrol SA (Colombia), 40 percent in AP Alternative Assets LP (the Netherlands), 38.9 percent in Banque de Tunisie et des Emirats (Tunisia), 25 percent in Arab International Bank (Egypt), 20 percent in Union Cement Company (UAE), and holdings in Joint Arab Investment Corporation (Egypt) and International Capital Trading (UAE).[48]

Year 2008 was perhaps the busiest year for ADIA. The most significant event in this year was the Citigroup deal discussed earlier. As it turned out, the investment was not as profitable as initially expected. However, ADIA continued to invest in other banks such as a 27.6 percent stake in Arab Banking Corporation (ABC).[49] It also turned over all its local and regional investment to ADIC and started to focus solely on foreign markets. ADIA was also active in the real estate sector of the emerging markets of Oceania. In January 2008, ADIA reportedly bought 19.9 percent of AMP NZ Office Trust (Anzo),[50] the largest listed office building owner, through its wholly–owned subsidiary (Haumi) from AMP Capital Investors[51] for $178.2 million.[52] In another interesting move in December 2008, ADIA entered into a partnership with Morgan Stanley (as the leader) and Allianz Capital Partners and formed the Chicago Parking Meters LLC. The joint venture leased more than 36,000 Chicago parking spaces for about $1.15 billion for 75 years until 2084. The

45   "Abu Dhabi Investment Authority Accumulates an 8% Stake in EFG-Hermes Holding," *Al Bawaba*, 21 May 2007.

46   Ares Management is an independent Los Angeles–based investment management firm. Established in 1997, assets under its management are estimated at about $29 billion.

47   Thornton and Reed, "A Power Player Emerges in the Gulf."

48   "Company Profile: Abu Dhabi Investment Authority," Zawya http://zawya.com/cm/profile.cfm/cid1000152/.

49   "S&P Reaffirms Rating for Arab Banking Corporation," *McClatchyTribune–The Middle East and North Africa Business Report*, 25 June 2008.

50   AMP NZ Office Trust is the New Zealand's largest investor in commercial office property. It has been listed on the New Zealand Stock Exchange since 1997 and has more than 7,000 investors.

51   AMP Capital Investors, based in Australia, is a wholly–owned subsidiary of AMP. It manages about $90 billion worth of assets.

52   "Abu Dhabi Buys Stake in Anzo," *The New Zealand Herald*, 18 January 2008.

deal became quite profitable after the partnership raised the parking rates several times since the lease began.[53]

As discussed, ADIA's investment is not confined to direct portfolio investment. The fund has acquired stakes in other companies indirectly and through its subsidiaries. In 1984, in a 50–50 joint venture with ADNOC, the International Petroleum Investment Company (IPIC) was established. The aim of IPIC was to focus on overseas oil–related acquisitions. Many of the IPIC board members are executives from ADIA and ADNOC. ADIA and ADNOC jointly make decisions about acquisitions by IPIC. ADIA analyzes deals based on their financial merits while ADNOC reviews its strategic importance with respect to Abu Dhabi's petroleum sector.[54] In September 2008, IPIC acquired $1.8 billion worth of convertible bonds of Aabar Investments.[55] This was the largest acquisition in the Middle East during that month. The total volume of mergers and acquisitions was $3.2 billion, the majority of which took place in Oman and United Arab Emirates.[56]

As discussed, ADIA's investment interest has reached many areas. In 2008, it announced that it was open to investment opportunities in Hong Kong. According to Ronald Arculli, executive counselor and chairman of the Hong Kong Exchanges and Clearing, "[t]hey agree that as a platform for investing on the mainland, Hong Kong is very suitable." He hoped that ADIA would establish an office in the city and said that the Hong Kong government would do anything to be accommodating.[57]

ADIA was interested in acquiring two shipyards in Poland. In early 2008, ADIA sent a query to the Polish Treasury and requested that a decision be made on the issue. Poland has been under pressure to privatize the shipyards in Szczecin and Gdynia, especially after the European Commission decided in July 2008 that shipyards had to return the subsidies they had received since 2004. The Gdansk shipyard was already privatized and controlled by Ukrainian–held ISD Polska. One of ADIA's directors, Abdul Aziz Abdullah al Ghurair, stated at the time: "We are interested in investing in Polish shipyards ... Poland should as soon as possible give us an offer convincing us of the benefits that we could gain from such a

---

53   Andrew Stern, "Chicago Leases Parking Meters for $1.16 Billion," *Reuters*, 2 December 2008; Darrell Preston, "Morgan Stanley's $11 Billion Makes Chicago Taxpayers Cry," *Bloomberg*, 9 August 2010.

54   "Abu Dhabi–the International Petroleum Investment Co," (APS Review Downstream Trends, 2001).

55   Aabar Petroleum Investments Company was established in 2005 focusing on oil and gas. In 2008, the company changed its name to Aabar Investments, sold its oil and gas subsidiary and became a diversified investment firm. In 2009, IPIC became a major shareholder of Aabar after the mandatory conversion of bonds purchased in 2008.

56   Nadia Saleem, "Slew of Mergers and Takeovers in Mena Region," *gulfnews.com*, 8 November 2008.

57   Dennis Eng, "Abu Dhabi's $650 USb Investment Arm Wooed," *South China Morning Post*, 1 February 2008.

transaction."[58] Despite its importance inside Poland, none of the deals for the two shipyards[59] went through and ADIA did not submit any offer[60] for undisclosed reasons.

Deutsche Bahn (DB) was also in discussion with ADIA (and other large investors in the region) regarding the public offering of one of DB's units. Hartmut Mehdorn, Chief Executive of DB, had held talks with large investors in the region on the possibility of listing about 25 percent of the DB Mobility Logistics AG unit in 2008. However, the offering was postponed due to the turmoil in the financial markets.[61]

In 2009, ADIA showed interest in the UK electricity distribution network of Electricité de France, which was offered for sale for about £4 million. In this deal, ADIA was competing against other interested buyers including Cheung Kong Infrastructure Holdings Ltd., Borealis Capital Corporation, Ontario Teachers' Pension Plan and CPP Investment Board, as well as the Scottish & Southern Energy plc, National Grid plc, Global Infrastructure Partners, and Morgan Stanley that intended to form a consortium to compete with the others.[62] The deal was, however, offered to a consortium led by a billionaire from Hong Kong in June 2010.[63]

The most recent activities of ADIA, in August 2010, includes taking part in an international investor group that has sought to buy the 110 km UK's high–speed rail that links London to the Channel Tunnel. Morgan Stanley and 3i are other ADIA's partners in this bid. The group will be competing against a group led by Groupe Eurotunnel SA (the Channel Tunnel operator) that includes Goldman Sachs Infrastructure Partners and Infracapital Partners (Prudential's infrastructure unit). [64]

Interestingly, while ADIA has been expanding in many directions, it has also remained selective about its investment choices on few occasions. For instance, in

---

58   "Abu Dhabi Invetment Authority Wants Offer for Polish Shipyards as Soon as Possible," *Poland Business Newswire*, 30 October 2008.

59   The Polish prime minister had previously said if the shipyards were not ceded by the end of August 2008, the Minister for Treasury would lose his position. Poland also received a second offer from the Qatar's largest investment bank, QInvest (one of the subsidiaries of the Qatari SWF). However, the QInvest dropped the offer on 1 September 2009. For more information see: "Poland Seeks New Shipyard Investor as QIA Stays Out," *Dow Jones Newswire*, 1 September 2009.

60   "Shipyards' Status Blocks Entry of Potential Investors," *Wasraw Business Journal*, 30 October 2008.

61   Kerstin Gehmlich, "D.Bahn IPO Unlikely This Year, Not Impossible: CEO," *Reuters*, 30 October 2008.

62   Danny Fortson, "EDF Attracts Big Hitters in Auction of £4bn UK Electricity Network," *The Sunday Times*, 16 August 2009.

63   "Abu Dhabi Fund Joins Morgan Stanley to Bid for UK Channel Tunnel Rail Link News," *domain-b.com*, 3 August 2010.

64   "Abu Dhabi Investment Authority Joins Morgan Stanley and 3i in UK Infrastructure Bid to Link London with the Channel Tunnel," *Invset in UK*, 2 August 2010.

1999 ADIA turned down the $310 million buyout of Champagne makers Mumm and Pierr–Jouet. Ultimately, the business was sold for $505 million to Allied Domecq in 2001.[65] Many believed the decision was based primarily on cultural and religious considerations, as the business involved alcohol. It also dropped the Polish shipyards deal discussed earlier for reasons not disclosed to the public, perhaps due to fears of political backlash. In another instance, ADIA—which had formally registered its interest in London's Gatwick airport[66]—dropped the deal in January 2009, when it failed to submit its initial bid by the deadline. Later in February 2010, ADIA acquired 15 percent stakes in Gatwick from Global Infrastructure Partners.[67] The overall expansion of ADIA in terms of its investment choices emphasizes the entrepreneurial aspect of its management.

State Entrepreneurship for Domestic Compensation

The United Arab Emirates is a young modern state, established only in the latter half of the twentieth century by small sheikhdoms. Although the formation of a government, appointment of its head, and administration (e.g., ministries and the national budget) take a modern political form, many of the major domestic political processes still follow the traditional values of the earlier sheikhdoms. Each emirate retains certain independence over its territory, resources, and budget. The status of a certain family or tribe still plays a great role in the running of both the local and federal governments. The influence and significance of the Al Nahyan family in the leadership of the country is evident. The formation of the United Arab Emirates itself as a modern state was initiated in the 1970s under the strong leadership of the ruler of Abu Dhabi, Sheikh Zayed bin Sultan Al Nahyan. This is what Davidson refers to as a "neopatrimonial model," with the executive branch entirely dominated by the members of the prominent families:

> Indeed, the presidency of the UAE is entirely synonymous with the traditional rulership of Abu Dhabi, the largest and wealthiest of the constituent emirates ... Moreover, with Abu Dhabi being by far the largest contributor to both the federal budget and the UAE's GDP, this historical association of the presidency with the ruler of Abu Dhabi has now been informally accepted by the other emirates.[68]

---

65   Thornton and Reed, "A Power Player Emerges in the Gulf."

66   David Robertson, "Sovereign Wealth Giant ADIA Drops out of Gatwick Race " *TimesOnline*, 20 January 2009.

67   "Abu Dhabi Fund Joins Morgan Stanley to Bid for UK Channel Tunnel Rail Link News."

68   Christopher M. Davidson, *The United Arab Emirates: A Study in Survival*, The Middle East in the International System (Boulder, Colo.: Lynne Rienner Publishers, 2005), 189.

Interestingly, both the Emirates' and ADIA's officials have asserted that the fund is primarily motivated by economic considerations. Even some local analysts strongly believe that ADIA is essentially an oil stabilization fund.[69] Nevertheless, ADIA remains one of the most opaque funds. Details of the fund's investments, assets under management, and decision–making processes remain a secret, despite ADIA's having been at the forefront of the development of the Santiago Principles for transparency and governance.

In effect, ADIA is managed by the ruler of Abu Dhabi (who is also the president of the Emirates) and the other board members appointed by the ruler, most of whom come from the Al Nahyan family. However, many of the day–to–day operations of the fund are managed by a number of western fund managers. For instance, until November 2008 the asset management in the Equity and Fixed–income Departments at ADIA was headed by Thomas Connelly, who had come from the Equity Research Department at Bear Sterns in New York City.[70] Another example is the appointment of Bill Schwab—a veteran of J.P. Morgan, Deutsche Bank, and Goldman Sachs—as the Global Head of Real Estate of ADIA in January 2009, making him responsible for the management of ADIA's global investment strategy in the real estate sector.[71] Despite presence of influential political figures on the board of directors, the actual management of the fund—to a great extent—remains non–political. The board effectively rejected few investment decisions, mainly due to cultural and religious considerations.

Both government and ADIA officials, on many occasions, have emphasized the commercial motive of the fund. For instance, Hamad Al Suwaidi, director of ADIA and Abu Dhabi Finance Department Secretary, stated: "One of the main principles of SWFs is to invest on an economic and financial risk–and–return basis. By law these funds will not be able to get involved in noncommercial activity …

---

69   For instance, Nadim Kawash, a reporter for Emirates Business 24|7, who has been extensively covering the issues surrounding ADIA, strongly believes that the fund is an oil stabilization fund that will protect both Abu Dhabi and the Emirates against a fall in oil prices. During our correspondence, he strongly discouraged me from looking into ADIA's investment behavior. His somewhat childish argument was that any such efforts are fruitless as the fund does not disclose any data, and that even those employed by ADIA do not have information on the operations of the fund. He further claimed that this issue is kept secret and discussed only during the annual meeting with Sheikh Zayed.

70   Connelly left ADIA in November 2008 to join BNY Melon Asset Management as the Bank's first head of asset management for the Middle East region. Source: "BNY Mellon Asset Managment Expands Middle East Regional Team," *Zawya*, 4 November 2008.

71   Schwab was with J.P. Morgan as a Managing Director in the European Real Estate Finance division, responsible for real estate transactions. He was also at the Deutsche Bank for five years as a Director in the Real Estate Capital Structure and Underwriting department. He was also a Chief Lending Officer in the Real Estate division at Goldman Sachs. Schwab also held numerous senior posts in real estate and construction industries. For more information see: "Press Release: Abu Dhabi Investment Authority Appoints Bill Schwab as Global Head of Real Estate," (Abu Dhabi Investment Authority, 2009).

By their very nature, sovereign wealth funds have a big stake in stable global financial markets."[72]

When most of the countries in the West became concerned about the agenda and investment approach of SWFs—especially those with little transparency—ADIA sent a letter to United States officials stressing that the government "will never use its investments as a foreign policy tool;" instead, the Emirate's sovereign funds "are similar to pension funds, combining a strong focus on long–term capital returns" to finance public services such as health care and infrastructure projects.[73] These statements also show the concerns on the part of ADIA's official with respect to the West perception of the fund's agenda.

Additionally, the available data on ADIA's investment does not indicate acquisition of shares in any politically–sensitive industries. Although not always successful, ADIA has invested in various instruments and industries across the globe and so far has avoided any areas that may be controversial, domestically (e.g., investment involving alcohol) or internationally (e.g., defense industries).

The history of ADIA's operation shows that the fund has consistently, but not always successfully, invested in industries that it deemed commercially and financially appropriate. Therefore, despite the structure and management of ADIA being greatly intertwined with political structures and the ruling family, there is no evidence that the fund was ever used to pursue political power through economic means.

ADIA has expanded its investment into different areas, and in doing so, it has mobilized all the resources at its disposal. Despite the fall in the value of the fund due to the global economic downturn, ADIA continued to acquire stakes in different companies and restructured its organization to focus solely on foreign markets. Additionally, the emphasis on equities in the portfolio shows that achieving high returns is a more immediate goal. As Setser and Ziemba have stated, ADIA is "viewing itself as a pure portfolio manager that seeks (not always successfully) the highest risk–adjusted return—not a fund that supports domestic or regional economic development."[74]

In the United Arab Emirates and the emirate of Abu Dhabi, there is a great emphasis on the role of the government in running the economy. This is mainly the legacy of the traditional and patriarchic structure of the society and the significance of the position of each ruler in running his emirate. This, in the context of the modern state, takes the form of state involvement in almost all areas. In fact, the major sectors of the economy are run by or regulated through the state–owned enterprises. For instance, the oil and gas industries, as well as investments related to this sector, are run by local state enterprises such as ADNOC or IPIC. Other public enterprises include Abu Dhabi Water and Electricity Authority (ADWEA),

---

72   "Wealth Funds' Long–Term View May Help Stablize Markets."

73   Rugaber, "Abu Dhabi Lays out Investment Principles for Its Government–Run Wealth Fund."

74   Setser and Ziemba, "GCC Sovereign Funds, Reversal of Fortune," 20.

Emirates Telecommunications Corporation (ETC), Dubai Ports World (global port operator), and Emaar Properties (the developer responsible for the world's tallest building—Burj Khalifa, formerly known as Burj Dubai).

All these considerations support the idea of state entrepreneurship in the case of ADIA. As discussed, the state entrepreneurial intervention through SOEs is an embedded characteristic of the United Arab Emirates, or in Gilpin's words, a unique feature of its "national system of political economy."[75] Additionally, the actual portfolio structure shows a greater concentration in riskier assets, highlighting the importance of profit maximization rather than maintaining the value of the income.

At the same time, the United Arab Emirates is a small state. It is highly dependent on its oil and gas resources and therefore, the price at which it is exporting the commodity. For the small Gulf economies "isolation and autarky were never viable options for achieving prosperity. These countries derive much of their income from exporting hydrocarbon resources to the world markets and invest considerable sums of these proceeds in international portfolio and direct investment."[76] Additionally, the Emirates' economy is particularly vulnerable to changes in global economic activity since it consists of a large services sector (e.g., shipping, banking, and tourism) that depend on the level of global economic activity.

Both the Abu Dhabi and United Arab Emirates budgets have a low tax base and therefore, are heavily dependent on the income from the export of oil and transfers from the Emirates' sovereign funds at times of economic hardship. According to its first annual report, ADIA is "a globally–diversified investment institution whose sole mission is to invest funds on behalf of the Government of the Emirate of Abu Dhabi to make available the necessary financial resources to secure and maintain the future welfare of the Emirate."[77] ADIA has—on several occasions—provided the government with funds and will continue to do so in the future, if need be. Moreover, as a non–democratic state, it may be necessary for the ruling regime to provide the few influential families with resources and wealth so as to ensure the continuity of the political system. In this case, ADIA can provide resources for such compensation in the long run.

In the case of ADIA, there is no evidence suggesting that the fund has been used as a foreign policy tool by either the federal government or the emirate of Abu Dhabi. The industries the fund has acquired stakes in are not politically sensitive, from a national security standpoint. Most of the investment is in the form of portfolio investment. Moreover, the fund's officials are aware of the created interdependencies and have been concerned about the security of the fund's own assets in recipient states. The

75   Robert Gilpin and Jean M. Gilpin, *Global Political Economy: Understanding the International Economic Order* (Princeton, N.J.: Princeton University Press, 2001).

76   *Gulf Oil and Gas: Ensuring Economic Security*, 1st ed. (Abu Dhabi: Emirates Center for Strategic Studies and Research, 2007), 57.

77   "Khalifa Names New Managing Director for Adia."

state intervention in the economy is also rooted in the traditional society of the emirates. Almost all of the main areas of the economy today are run or regulated by the government. The wide range of financial instruments as well as the greater emphasis on equities in the portfolio of ADIA indicates that the fund's agenda is focused on generating profit and diversification of assets as a risk management tool. At the same time, the fund's resources (or returns) provide sources of income for the federal budget and are therefore used as a social bargain. The conclusion is that the state entrepreneurship argument provides the most relevant and applicable context for the operation of ADIA. At the same time, the domestic compensation argument provides additional insights into the formation and purpose of the fund. In the United Arab Emirates, state entrepreneurship—as embodied in ADIA—is aimed at providing required resources for domestic compensation.

Lack of transparency, nevertheless, remains one of the main challenges to the micro–level study of ADIA. In fact, Emirates' authorities may have perceived secrecy as an entrepreneurial tactic for the success of the fund. As Barbary and Chin put it, "money and mystery are a potent mix, and this enabled ADIA to attract some of the best asset managers in the business ... This has been critical to its success."[78] Lack of transparency and disclosure may also be a cultural issue or simply indicate underdeveloped standards and procedures.

---

78   Barbary and Chin, "Testing Time, Sovereign Wealth Funds in the Middle East & North Africa and the Global Financial Crisis," 38.

References

"Abu Dhabi–the International Petroleum Investment Co." APS Review Downstream Trends, 2001.

"Abu Dhabi Buys Stake in Anzo." *The New Zealand Herald*, 18 January 2008.

"Abu Dhabi Fund Joins Morgan Stanley to Bid for UK Channel Tunnel Rail Link News." *domain-b.com*, 3 August 2010.

"Abu Dhabi Investment Authority Accumulates an 8% Stake in EFG-Hermes Holding." *Al Bawaba*, 21 May 2007.

"Abu Dhabi Investment Authority Joins Morgan Stanley and 3i in UK Infrastructure Bid to Link London with the Channel Tunnel." *Invset in UK*, 2 August 2010.

"Abu Dhabi Invetment Authority Wants Offer for Polish Shipyards as Soon as Possible." *Poland Business Newswire*, 30 October 2008.

Al–Otaiba, Yousef. "Our Sovereign Wealth Plans." *The Wall Street Journal*, 10 March 2008, A16.

Barbary, Victoria, and Edward Chin. "Testing Time, Sovereign Wealth Funds in the Middle East & North Africa and the Global Financial Crisis." London: Monitor Company Group L.P., 2009.

"BNY Mellon Asset Managment Expands Middle East Regional Team." *Zawya*, 4 November 2008.

Campbell, Dankin, and Andrew MacAskill. "Abu Dhabi Fund Seeks to End Citigroup Share Purchase." *Bloomberg*, 16 December 2009.

"Citigroup to Sell 47.5 Billion in Equity Units to Abu Dhabi Investment Authority." *The Associated Press*, 27 November 2007.

"Company Profile: Abu Dhabi Investment Authority." Zawya http://zawya.com/cm/profile.cfm/cid1000152/.

Davidson, Christopher M. *The United Arab Emirates: A Study in Survival*, The Middle East in the International System. Boulder, Colo.: Lynne Rienner Publishers, 2005.

Eng, Dennis. "Abu Dhabi's $650 USb Investment Arm Wooed." *South China Morning Post*, 1 February 2008.

England, Andrew. "ADIA Makes Play for a Native Minority." *Financial Times*, 16 November 2008.

Fortson, Danny. "EDF Attracts Big Hitters in Auction of £4bn UK Electricity Network." *The Sunday Times*, 16 August 2009.

Gehmlich, Kerstin. "D.Bahn IPO Unlikely This Year, Not Impossible: CEO." *Reuters*, 30 October 2008.

Gilpin, Robert, and Jean M. Gilpin. *Global Political Economy: Understanding the International Economic Order*. Princeton, N.J.: Princeton University Press, 2001.

Gulf Oil and Gas: Ensuring Economic Security. 1st ed. Abu Dhabi: Emirates Center for Strategic Studies and Research, 2007.

Karmin, Craig, and Carolyn Cui. "Smart–Money Bets on Street Turn Sour-Big Investors Find Some Big Losses; 'Stakes on the Cheap'." *The Wall Street Journal*, 19 September 2008.

Kawach, Nadim. "Bond Issues to Help Boost UAE." *Emirates Business 24|7*, 3 May 2009.

———. "UAE's Overseas Invetsmnet Income to Rebound in 2009." *Emirates Business 24|7*, 20 April 2009.

Kaye, Daniel. "UAE Money Data Reveals Financial System under Stress." National Bank of Kuwait, 2009.

"Khalifa Names New Managing Director for Adia." *Gulfnews.com*, 14 April 2010.

Peck, Malcolm C. *The United Arab Emirates: A Venture in Unity*, Profiles. Nations of the Contemporary Middle East. Boulder, Colo.: Westview Press, 1986.

"Poland Seeks New Shipyard Investor as QIA Stays Out." *Dow Jones Newswire*, 1 September 2009.

"Press Release: Abu Dhabi Investment Authority Appoints Bill Schwab as Global Head of Real Estate." Abu Dhabi Investment Authority, 2009.

Preston, Darrell. "Morgan Stanley's $11 Billion Makes Chicago Taxpayers Cry." *Bloomberg*, 9 August 2010.

Remo-Listana, Karen. "Wealth Funds in the UAE Lead Way with Transparency." *Emirates Business 24|7*, 3 March 2009.

Robertson, David. "Sovereign Wealth Giant ADIA Drops out of Gatwick Race " *TimesOnline*, 20 January 2009.

Rugaber, Christopher S. "Abu Dhabi Lays out Investment Principles for Its Government–Run Wealth Fund." *The Associated Press*, 18 March 2008.

Rugh, Andrea B. *The Political Culture of Leadership in the United Arab Emirates*. New York: Palgrave Macmillan, 2007.

"S&P Reaffirms Rating for Arab Banking Corporation." *McClatchyTribune–The Middle East and North Africa Business Report*, 25 June 2008.

Saleem, Nadia. "Slew of Mergers and Takeovers in Mena Region." *gulfnews.com*, 8 November 2008.

Setser, Brad, and Rachel Ziemba. "GCC Sovereign Funds, Reversal of Fortune." New York: Council on Foreign Relations, Center for Geoeconomic Studies, 2009.

"Shipyards' Status Blocks Entry of Potential Investors." *Wasraw Business Journal*, 30 October 2008.

Stern, Andrew. "Chicago Leases Parking Meters for $1.16 Billion." *Reuters*, 2 December 2008.

Thornton, Emily, and Stanley Reed. "A Power Player Emerges in the Gulf." *BusinessWeek*, no. 4089 (2008): 63-64.

"The UAE Economy: Sustainable in the Face of a Serious Global Recession ". Riadh: Samba Financial Group, 2009.

"Wealth Funds' Long–Term View May Help Stablize Markets." *IMF Survey*, 16 October 2008.

Zahlan, Rosemarie Said. *The Making of the Modern Gulf States: Kuwait, Bahrain, Qatar, the United Arab Emirates, and Oman.* Rev. and updated ed. Reading, Berkshire, U.K.: Ithaca Press, 1998.

Chapter 5
How Singapore's Temasek Transformed State's Economic Management

The third SWF case study looks at Singapore's Temasek[1] Holdings. Temasek, which was established more than 35 years ago, has a number of characteristics that make it unique in a number of ways. Unlike the majority of SWFs, which are funded by excess foreign reserves or proceeds from the export of the abundant resource (typically oil) and invest their money in foreign portfolio, Temasek was initially endowed with a portfolio of companies that was placed under its management by the Singapore Ministry of Finance. While other government agencies manage the extensive surpluses generated by the budget sector or the balance of payments, Temasek manages the government's stakes in various companies at home and abroad.

Another interesting feature of Temasek is the unique nature of the relationship between its management and the President of Singapore. The president is in fact the financial guardian of Singapore assets and the only person whose concurrence is needed for appointment or removal of the Board of Directors of Temasek. Furthermore, Temasek is the first SWF to issue bonds in the same way private corporations issue bonds to finance their business.

Today Temasek is the biggest shareholder in half of Singapore's largest (by market value) publicly traded companies.[2] Many of its foreign investments have been made through a sophisticated network of fully–owned subsidiaries or joint ventures. As will be discussed, Temasek has acted mainly as the entrepreneurial arm of the government and has strived to provide assistance to local communities or mobilize resources in case of natural disasters. But more importantly, Temasek has facilitated the process of privatization and has actively managed the state's equities in various business areas ranging from banking and finance to manufacturing and technology with very little, if any, cash position or risk–free assets.

Temasek is categorized as a transparent fund, based on L–M Transparency Index. It has published annual reviews disclosing its group financials since 2006, and has been relatively open to outside enquiries. There is, however, little information about the management and performance of Temasek during the period between its inception and the turn of the century. Additionally, the relationship between the fund and the national budget is not entirely clear and so is the relationship

---

1   Temasek means sea town. It was also the original name of Singapore.
2   Simon Bennett, "Temasek's Mapletree Plans to List S\$4 Billion REIT," *Bloomberg*, 12 September 2009.

between its board of directors, the management of its portfolio companies, and the government. Temasek has, nevertheless, been sensitive to public opinion and has used every opportunity to respond to misperceptions held by outsiders, including the general public as well as policy makers.

As will be discussed, there is no evidence indicating that the fund, which is relatively illiquid and reflects an above–average tolerance for risk, was established or has ever been used as a precautionary means for coping with external financial shocks or domestic liquidity shortages. There is certainly a need for domestic compensation mechanisms or precautionary saving deposits in a small state that is also highly interdependent with the global economy (and therefore vulnerable) like Singapore; however, Temasek was not intended to serve such purpose.

Not an Ordinary Sovereign Fund

The creation of Temasek is closely linked to the history and structure of the Singapore economy and the role of the state in economic development. It is important to know that the core of the Singapore economic system was formed in response to numerous political and economic challenges. Singapore in its modern form is a young state, somewhat similar to the United Arab Emirates. Before declaring its independence, Singapore was a part of the British Empire. In 1942 it fell to Japan but was recaptured in 1945 by the British army. Singapore became a part of the Federation of Malaysia[3] in September 1963. Regional political tensions and specifically the growing tension with the Malay leaders, forced Singapore to declare independence on 9 August 1965. Since then the People Actions Party (PAP) has been in control of the government and has remained the dominant political party in Singapore.

Not too long after independence in 1968, the British government abandoned its naval base due to the high costs of maintaining the facility. This meant a massive job loss for the local people, whose livelihoods depended on the British facility. In a process generally explained by Toynbee's "challenge and response"[4] thesis, the economy of Singapore was shaped in reaction to a series of major misfortunes in the early years of independence. Between 1966 and 1973, "Singapore was in its 'heroic' phase of growth, moving along at the impressive rate of 12.3 percent a

---

3   Federation of Malaysia was composed of the former Federation of Malaya, Singapore, Sabah, and Sarawak.

4   Toynbee's argument was that minor challenges do not induce any responses. A significant and sizable challenge, however, can produce industrial development. For further information see Alexander Gerschenkron and Seymour Martin Lipset collection., *Economic Backwardness in Historical Perspective, a Book of Essays* (Cambridge, Mass.: Belknap Press of Harvard University Press, 1962), 11; Jurgen Schmandt and C. H. Ward, *Sustainable Development: The Challenge of Transition* (Cambridge, U.K.: Cambridge University Press, 2000).

year."[5] Although economic growth rate fell afterwards, it still remained well above the growth rate of the industrial states. Immediately after the independence, the government realized that the strategy of import substitution was not viable since the domestic market was too small. Therefore, tariffs and quotas were reduced and an export promotion strategy was adopted in the late 1960s.

The government also recognized the need for both physical infrastructure and the institutions required for economic growth. It therefore took the lead in managing the economy, especially in areas where private players were absent. The government even set up enterprises in competition with the private sector. According to Lim et al.:

> Besides being the exclusive provider of infrastructure and social services, as are many other governments, the Singapore government engaged in direct production. The main reason for doing so in the 1960s was to build large, high–risk enterprises, such as the National Iron and Steel Mills and Jurong Shipyard. The government also set up state–owned companies to take over some functions from public agencies that had grown too rapidly with a view of safeguarding institutional efficiency and flexibility ... By the early 1980s the government owned close to 450 companies in a wide range of manufacturing and service industries...[6]

The government, and specifically the Deputy Prime Minister, Dr. Goh Keng Swee, believed that there was no choice but to ensure that government investments were commercially sound and sustainable. Dr. Goh Keng Swee, who is also regarded as the architect of Singapore's modernization and economic development, believed that the task of managing various economic entities should be in the hands of managers other than the government bureaucrats. He asserts his view clearly by saying: "One of the tragic illusions that many countries of the Third World entertain is the notion that politicians and civil servants can successfully perform entrepreneurial functions. It is curious that, in the face of overwhelming evidence to the contrary, the belief persists."[7]

Against this background, Temasek Holdings was established on 25 June 1974 by the government of Singapore to take over the ownership and management of 35 government–linked companies (GLCs) whose shares were held by the Singapore Ministry of Finance. "The objective was to find a way to better manage the portfolio

---

5   Linda Lim, Pang Eng Fong, and Ronald Findlay, "Five Small Open Economies," in *A World Bank Comparative Study. The Political Economy of Poverty, Equity, and Growth.*, ed. Ronald Findlay and Stanislaw Wellisz (New York: Published for the World Bank [by] Oxford University Press, 1993), 97.

6   Ibid., 108.

7   Quoted in The Committee on Financial Services, United States House of Representatives, *Testimony by Simon Israel, Temasek Holdings: A Dependable Investor in the United States*, 5 March 2008.

of companies and investments accumulated by the Ministry of Finance in the first decade of nation building since 1965."[8] The establishment of Temasek is unique in the sense that, unlike most of the SWFs, it was not funded by foreign reserves or balance of trade surpluses. Instead, Temasek received its initial endowment of S\$345 million (about \$134 million) in the form of company stock from the Ministry of Finance.

Temasek was not designed to provide resources for balance of payment correction, although the Singapore's current account balance was constantly in deficit in the 1970s and early 1980s. The deficit was mostly corrected through the financial account. In the early 1990s and concurrent with the global waves of liberalization, the government of Singapore transferred additional state–owned companies to Temasek. The fund took over companies such as SingTel (telecommunications), Port of Singapore Authority (PSA) International (the world's second largest port operators), and SingPower (power generation).

Temasek has been governed under the Singapore Companies Act, which requires that directors have the fiduciary duty of acting in the best interest of the shareholders. In accordance with Chapter 50 of the Act, Temasek Holdings is considered an exempt company and is therefore not required to publish audited statutory consolidated financial statements.[9] In 1991, the Singapore Constitution was revised and Temasek was designated as a Fifth Schedule Company. The revision also granted the President of Singapore more roles than his previous ceremonial role. The President (now appointed by popular vote instead of the Parliament, for a period of six years) became the "fiscal guardian" of Temasek and other Fifth Schedule companies.[10] This meant that the President's approval was required for spending past reserves, including those accumulated by Temasek and other Fifth Schedule companies. The President could also veto the budget if he believed that it put the past reserves at risk.[11] This also meant that the government could not withdraw from the assets under the management of Temasek or other Fifth Schedule companies for its own purpose. Many believed that it was very important for the President to have "an independent and direct

---

8   "Frequently Asked Questions About Temasek Holdings," Temasek Holdings, http://www.temasekholdings.com.sg/pdf/TemasekHoldingsFAQs.pdf.

9   According to the Chapter 50 of the Singapore Companies Act, an exempt company has no more than 20 shareholders, none of which are corporate, and is not required to file its audited financial statements with the public registry.

10   Other Fifth Schedule entities include Singapore's Government Investment Corporation (GIC), which manages the reserves of the government, Central Provident Fund (CPF), a pension fund or a mandatory saving scheme financed by payroll contributions, and the Monetary Authority of Singapore (MAS), which acts as the central bank.

11   This is also referred to as "two–key" principle, meaning both the Parliament (government) and the President have to agree in order to use the past reserves.

electoral mandate in order to be in a position to legitimately overrule the will of Parliament (government)."[12]

It took Temasek almost 28 years to issue its Charter. The Charter, issued on 3 July 2002, stated that Temasek "holds and manages the Singapore Government's investment in companies, for the long term benefit of Singapore,"[13] with a focus on value (profit) creation and the maximization of customer fulfillment and shareholder (Ministry of Finance) returns. The Charter refers to the various types of businesses that are managed by Temasek. These include companies that are critical to Singapore's security or economic welfare, natural monopolies (e.g., water, power, gas, and airport operations), and businesses that have a potential for becoming internationalized.[14] In 2009, the Charter was revised and re–written, and corporate citizenship was added to Temasek's responsibilities, while key concepts such as the maximization of shareholder value, active investment, and consistent value creation remained unchanged.

The first annual report, called the Temasek Review, was published in 2006, and stated that the mission of the fund was to create and maximize long–term shareholder value as an active investor and shareholder of successful enterprises."[15] Today, Temasek Holdings employs about 380 people from 24 countries in more than ten different offices around the globe.[16] As of 31 March 2010, the portfolio under its management amounted to S$186 billion ($132 billion) and has delivered an annual compounded total shareholder return of about 16 percent since its inception in 1974.[17] The sources of financing for Temasek are dividends from the portfolio companies, proceeds from divestment, and the occasional transfer of new companies by the Ministry of Finance. Temasek has a corporate credit rating of AAA and Aaa by Standard and Poor's (S&P) and Moody's respectively.

Temasek is led by an eleven–member Board of Directors and a senior management team that includes a few western business executives.[18] It also benefits from the insight and advice of several Board committees, an international panel as well as several advisory panels that consist of business leaders from around

12   Jón R. Blöndal, "Budgeting in Singapore," (Organisation for Economic Co–operation and Development, 2006), 20.

13   Tommy T. B. Koh and Li Lin Chang, *The United States-Singapore Free Trade Agreement: Highlights and Insights* (Singapore: World Scientific Pub; Institute of Policy Studies, 2004), 258.

14   Ibid., 260-61.

15   "Temasek Review 2006," (Temasek Holdings, 2006), 11.

16   In addition to the head office in Singapore, Temasek has five offices in China, two in India and Vietnam each, and new offices in Brazil and Mexico.

17   "Temasek Review 2010," (Temasek Holdings, 2010).

18   For instance, Simon Israel—a ten–veteran of Danone Group—has served as both a board member and a member of the senior management team since 2005. Marcus Wallenberg—Chairman of the Skandinaviska Enskilda Banken and a few other major corporations—also joined the Board of Directors in 2008. In August 2010, Gregory Curl—former chief risk officer at the Bank of America—joined the senior management team.

the world. The Board of Directors is currently constituted of 11 members who also serve as board members or are on the management team of other companies affiliated with Temasek. The Board has been chaired by S Dhanabalan since September 1996. He is a former cabinet member (1978–1994) and has been the chairman of a number of companies, including DBS Group and Singapore Airlines, in which Temasek has 28 percent and 54 percent stakes respectively.

The Chief Executive Officer (CEO) and the Executive Director of Temasek is Ho Ching, the wife of the current Singapore Prime Minister, Lee Hsien Loong. She has been the Executive Director since May 2002 and the CEO since January 2004. Ho Ching held positions in the defense industry and was the president and CEO of the Singapore Technologies Group before joining Temasek. In early 2009, Temasek was set to name Charles "Chip" Goodyear as the first foreign national CEO of the fund.[19] This was viewed as a step toward greater transparency and professionalism. However, on 20 July 2009, Temasek unexpectedly announced that the plan for the leadership transfer would not proceed due to "differences regarding certain strategic issues that could not be resolved."[20]

Goodyear reportedly was expected to change the fund's strategy and shift the focus from financial investments to natural resources.[21] There were also reports that Goodyear was trying to instill a greater degree of discipline and that he "had fired people for showing up late to internal meetings and had prohibited them from typing messages on their BlackBerry's during meetings."[22] Temasek officials offered very little explanation for this decision, but indicated that the search for a well–qualified CEO would continue. Nevertheless, Temasek has not appointed a new CEO even after a year.

According to the Temasek Review, the Board of Directors and the management team are responsible for business decisions related to investment or divestment. The fund asserts that neither the President of Singapore nor the Ministry of Finance can get involved in the operations of Temasek, while the former safeguards the assets under management of Temasek from the latter's potential withdrawal for budgetary purposes. The Board of Directors provides the overall policy direction to the management team. The management of Temasek claims that it complies with the local rules and regulations pertaining to its investment or operation and has no involvement in the day–to–day operations of the portfolio companies. It gets involved only in the capacity of a shareholder exercising its rights and voting at shareholders' meetings.

---

19   Charles Goodyear is the U.S. born former head of BHP Billiton (Australian mining company). He joined the Temasek's Board of Directors on 1 February 2009, and was to replace Ho Ching in October 2009.

20   "Temasek and Transparency–II," *The Wall Street Journal*, 21 July 2009.

21   John Burton, "Temasek and US's Goodyear Part Ways," *Financial Times*, 22 July 2009.

22   Fiona Chan, "Goodyear Rumors 'Far from the Truth'," *AsiaOne*, 1 August 2009.

One of the interesting features of Temasek is the unique nature of the relationship between the fund's Board of Directors and management on the one hand and the President of Singapore on the other hand. As mentioned earlier, after the revision of the Constitution in 1991, the President's role changed from a ceremonial one to one of a financial guardian of Singapore's assets (including past reserves). The appointment or removal of Board members by the Ministry of Finance (the sole shareholder of the fund) is subject to the President's concurrence.

Additionally, the President is responsible for preserving the country's fiscal discipline and protecting the accumulated national reserves. Any profits or assets built up during a previous government term are considered past reserves and become untouchable once a new government is in power. Any deficit or negative reserves should be corrected using the reserves accumulated within the current government term. In other words, the government can run a deficit only if it has already built up surpluses during its five–year term. In order to draw on the past reserves, approval of both the President and the Parliament must be obtained.[23] This also indicates that Temasek assets cannot be used for balance of payments corrections.

Due to its exempt status, information about Temasek Holdings, including its financial statements between 1974 and 2000, is not available and only a summary of data for financial years 2002 to 2004 is included in the first Temasek Review which was issued in 2006. Temasek was, however, subject to financial audits and has received international ratings. The consolidated financial statements of Temasek Holdings have, at least since financial year 2001, been examined by either of the two major accounting and auditing firms (i.e., PricewaterhouseCoopers and KPMG) whose auditors' reports contained unqualified opinions.[24]

There is a wide spectrum of industries that Temasek Holdings invests in. These include banking and financial services, transportation, infrastructure, real estate, telecommunications, and energy. Temasek manages its portfolio of different companies by exercising its shareholder rights to influence the general direction of the companies, allegedly without getting involved in the day–to–day business operations and decisions. Over the past few years, the composition of the portfolio in terms of its exposure to geographical areas and markets has changed. As Table 5.1 shows, the market value of the portfolio has grown steadily, albeit with the exception of financial year 2008–09 during which all assets were impacted by the global financial crisis. As can be seen in the table, the geographical focus of the portfolio has also shifted from domestic and OECD markets to regional and emerging markets.

---

23   The President can also veto the government budget if he is of the opinion that such budget entails the risk of using past reserves.

24   For financial years 2001–02 to 2006–07, PriceWaterHouseCoopers conducted the audit. KPMG audited the consolidated financial statements for the financial years 2007–08 and 2008–09.

Table 5.1   Temasek portfolio by market value and geographical distribution (financial year ending 31 March)

	2003–04	2004–05	2005–06	2006–07	2007–08	2008–09	2009–10
Market Value (S$ billion)	90	103	129	164	185	130	186
Geography (percent)							
Singapore	52	49	44	38	33	31	32
Asia (excluding Singapore)	16	19	34	40	43	43	46
OECD	32	30	20	20	23	22	20
Latin America and Others *	0	2	2	2	3	4	2

Sources: Temasek Reviews 2006, Temasek Review 2008, Temasek Review 2009, and Temasek Review 2010

* Mexico was classified under OECD in 2004 and later included in Latin America and Others.

Since 2004, emphasis on domestic market has been lessened and has shifted instead to North Asia, Latin America and other regions. The portfolio structure is divided almost equally between emerging markets (characterized by higher risks) and developed countries (characterized by slower growth rates and lower risks). The Chairman of the Board of Directors, S. Dhanabalan, has clearly indicated the fund's approach with respect to risk, saying: "[A]s Asia continues to make progress, it will continue to de–risk. We are comfortable to maintain an overweight in Asia ..."[25]

Table 5.2 shows the changes in the portfolio by sector since financial year 2004. As can be seen, a large portion of the portfolio consists of companies active in the financial sector, telecommunication, and media. However, over time the emphasis has shifted from telecommunication and infrastructure to financial services and new areas such as life science and consumers. After the recent global financial crises, Temasek reduced its exposure to the financial services sector. During financial year 2008–09, Temasek took advantage of lower asset prices and strengthened its portfolio position in real estate, transportation, and logistics. By the end of March 2010, Temasek had increased its exposure to financial services to 37 percent while reducing its position in telecommunications, media, transportation, and industries sectors.[26]

25   "Temasek Review 2009," (Temasek Holdings, 2009), 12.
26   "Temasek Review 2010," 17.

Table 5.2   Temasek portfolio by sector (percent, financial year ending 31 March)

	2004	2005	2006	2007	2008	2009
Financial Services	21	21	35	38	40	33
Telecommunication and Media	36	33	26	23	24	26
Transportation and Logistics	14	17	13	12	10	13
Infrastructure, Engineering & Technology	10	10	9	8	8	7
Real Estate	6	8	7	9	7	9
Energy and Resources	7	8	6	6	5	5
Others	6	3	4	4	6	7

Sources: Temasek Review 2006, Temasek Review 2008, and Temasek Review 2009

Another distinctive feature of Temasek is the issuance of bonds in order to finance its operations. Initially, the information on the bond holdings of the fund was not available to people residing in the United States. In October 2009 Temasek removed the restriction and information about bond issues became available to the wider public.[27] In September 2005, Temasek issued $1.75 billion worth of ten–year bonds with a coupon rate of 4.5 percent. In late October 2009, Temasek took advantage of low interest rates and raised another $1.5 billion through its wholly–owned subsidiary Temasek Financial Ltd. in order to "provide the net proceeds from the offering to Temasek and its subsidiary companies to fund their ordinary course of business."[28] The second series of the ten–year bonds carried a 4.3 percent coupon and was jointly put on the market by Deutsche Bank AG, Goldman Sachs Group Inc., and Morgan Stanley. In November 2009, Temasek issued the third series of US dollar denominated bonds with the total value of $0.5 billion. This was followed by five further issues of bonds, denominated in Singaporean dollar, with a total value of S$2.6 billion. The bonds maturity ranged between ten and 30 years.[29]

Steering Through Bust and Boom

As a small open economy, Singapore has been vulnerable to adverse international economic developments. In fact, the country has already endured a number of international crises. The first oil crisis induced a recession in 1974 and 1975 and resulted in shrinkage of the export sector and mass layoffs of workers in this sector.

---

27   This temporary restriction was most likely due to the fact that Temasek was planning to issues a second series of bond in late October 2009.

28   Ditas Lopez, "Temasek Looks to Tap U.S. Bond Markets," *The Wall Street Journal,* 20 October 2009, C2.

29   "Temasek Review 2010," 32.

During the 1985–86 recession, which was due in part to high wages in the exports sector and the reduced demand for electronic products, the Singapore dollar also came under speculative pressure. Since then, the government has reduced emphasis on high tech. During the East Asian financial crisis of 1997, which began with the floating of the Thai baht, Singapore first used the exchange rate policy, allowing a gradual 20 percent depreciation in the Singapore dollar to fight the recession. Later as the crisis dragged into 1998, Singapore focused on wage controls and cost–cutting initiatives to maintain the health of its economy.

Much of Singapore's success in managing the crises is due to the effective monetary and exchange rate policy as well as wage and cost controls rather than to fiscal policy. In this process, Singapore has mainly relied on institutions such as the Central Provident Fund (CPF) or the Government Investment Corporation (GIC).[30] Temasek did not seem to play a major role during the past crises either, a perception that is supported by the fact that its investment income was excluded from the government budget. The recent mortgage crisis provides an opportunity, however limited, to examine the role that Temasek may have played in the government's efforts to cope with the crisis. But before that, an overview of the relationship between Temasek and the government budget is necessary.

As mentioned earlier, Temasek is a holding company that manages a portfolio of state–owned companies for the government. In other words, it manages shares owned by the government. During the early years of Temasek, most of its portfolio consisted of domestic companies. The goal was to make the portfolio companies internationally competitive. Later when this task was lessened, Temasek managed to expand its operations (portfolio management) to include overseas companies. This was achieved through portfolio investment, mergers and acquisitions (M&A), and joint ventures.

The government is entitled to dividends from owned companies. Temasek's dividends are based on its net profit and the realized capital gains or losses from its investments. Up until the year 2000, Singapore's focus was on fiscal discipline and sustainability, which was achieved by excluding the use of investment income. The government used the "operating revenue," which did not include investment income. The only sources of revenue were taxes and fees. "In 2000, Singapore's budget concepts were revised and parts of net investment income derived from investments of past surpluses were now treated for budgetary purposes. This was an implicit recognition of the tight fiscal realities."[31]

In January 2001, in response to fiscal contractions, the Constitutional Amendment Bill was passed. The Bill allowed the government to use up to 50 percent of the Net Investment Income (NII). As a result, the income (dividends)

---

30   The CPF is financed by payroll contributions, which are invested in government securities. This arrangement allows the members to withdraw funds for items such as housing, retirement, and medical expenses. The GIC is the government's fund manager for official reserves.

31   Blöndal, "Budgeting in Singapore," 8.

from companies managed by Temasek, as well as investment income from GIC and Monetary Authority of Singapore (MAS), was included as a revenue item in the budget as Net Investment Income Contribution (NIIC).[32]

Singapore's economy also contracted after the recent sub–prime mortgage crisis. Similar to other governments that had introduced rescue packages and adopted expansionary policies—and also in light of the increasing future government expenditures—Singapore passed another amendment to the Constitution in January 2008. The amendment introduced the concept of "long–term expected returns" and permitted the government to use up to 50 percent of these returns. The critical issue is that Temasek was excluded from the new arrangement—i.e., access to the long–term expected returns (effective 1 January 2009) was limited to the MAS, which manages the official reserves of Singapore, as well as GIC.

Interestingly, in adapting this concept the Ministry of Finance drew upon the Norwegian experience and Norway's inclusion of the expected real return on the Government Pension Fund–Global of Norway in the budget in the aftermath of the recent crisis.[33] The Minister for Finance, Tharman Shanmugaratnam provided a number of reasons for this decision:

> The nature of Temasek's investment strategy ... involves taking concentrated stakes in companies, including direct investments. Like other such investors, this strategy entails higher risks, with the expectation of higher returns ... this approach makes it more difficult for us to project a long–term expected rate of return on Temasek's portfolio to a reasonable degree of certainty ... Temasek's investment strategy is still evolving, having begun a major effort to diversify its investments geographically and sectorally in 2002. Temasek today operates very differently from the way it was operating six years ago, and its strategy will continue to evolve in response to the investment climate ... It will therefore be prudent to leave Temasek out of the new framework.[34]

The statement clearly shows that Temasek's focus is on maximizing returns, which automatically entails higher risk. Because of this risk, the government is not ready to include the fund into its budget that requires conservative planning. Temasek, like many other funds and businesses, sustained losses during the crisis. The market value of Temasek's portfolio dropped significantly from S$185 billion in the financial year ending March 2008 to S$130 billion at the end of March 2009.

---

32   NII refers to the dividends, interest and other income received from investing reserves, as well as interest received from loans, after deducting management and administration expenses. NIIC is a part of NII that is taken into the budget to augment the Government's revenues. For more information see "Budget Highlights, Financial Year 2009: Keeping Jobs, Building for the Future," (Singapore Ministry of Finance, 2009).

33   "Second Reading Speech for Constitution of Republic of Singapore (Amendment) Bill 2008," (Singapore Ministry of Finance 2008).

34   Ibid., 27-28.

Similarly, the profit margin, expressed as a percentage of revenue, dropped from 24.2 percent to only nine percent during the same period.[35]

Despite the tough market, Temasek continued to actively manage its portfolio. During 2008 and early 2009, Temasek divested about S$16 billion of its assets and invested S$9 billion in new assets, including S$3 billion of rights offerings[36] of its portfolio companies.[37] In fact, Temasek managed to complete the 14–year long process of the privatization of the Singapore's power generation sector, which produced 90 percent of the country's power. It sold Tuas Power to SinoSing Power (a wholly owned subsidiary of China Huaneng Group)[38] for S$4.24 billion ($3 billion).[39] This was followed by the sale of Senoko Power to Lion Power Holdings (a consortium led by Japanese Marubeni Corporation) for S$3.65 billion ($2.40 billion) and the sale of PowerSeraya to YLT Power International of Malaysia for about S$3.11 billion (all three companies for a total of S$11 billion).[40]

Since the start of the recent financial crisis, Temasek has divested a significant amount of its stakes in the financial sector, most likely as a result of the not so bright horizon for the financial system and financial products. Temasek sold its entire stakes in Bank Internasional Indonesia (BII) which it held since 2003, Merrill Lynch (held since 2007)[41], Barclays (held since 2007), China Minsheng Banking Corporation (held since 2004)[42], and E.SUN Financial Holding Company (held since 2006). As a result, the allocation of financial services companies in Temasek's portfolio dropped from 40 percent to 33 percent between 2008 and 2009 (see Table 5.2).

Temasek also shifted its focus from Western markets to Asian and emerging markets (including those in South America) and increased its investment in real estate, transportation, and logistics sectors. In September 2008, Temasek invested about S$700 million in Li & Fung, a global supply chain management company

---

35   "Temasek Review 2009."
36   In a rights offering or issue, a company sells new shares at a discounted price to its existing investors to raise capital.
37   "Temasek Review 2009."
38   Ibid.
39   "Singapore: Temasek to Sell Electricity Generator," *Mysinchew.com*, 8 October 2008.
40   "Singapore Temasek to Sell Power Firm PowerSeraya," *Xinhua*, 7 October 2008.
41   Temasek initially acquired 9.4 percent stakes in Merrill Lynch in December 2007 and later raised it to 13.7 percent to become the largest shareholder in September 2008. On 1 January 2009, Merrill was acquired by Bank of America. By end of March 2009, Temasek sold all its shares in Bank of America at a significant loss. Merrill had to pay Temasek $2.5billion to offset losses Temasek incurred after acquiring share in December 2007. For further information see "Merill Posts 3rd–Quarter Loss of $5.2 Billion," *The New York Times*, 16 October 2008.
42   The Minsheng divestment was mainly due to regulatory reasons, based on which Temasek could not hold share in more than two Chinese banks. Temasek has stakes in China Construction Bank Corporation and Bank of China Limited.

providing service for major brands and retailers.[43] In October, Temasek, through its real estate arm (Mapletree Investments), entered into a contract to develop a $400 million, 75–hectare business park in Binh Duong Province in Vietnam. Mapletree is also involved in the development of several logistics parks in Vietnam.[44] In June 2009, Temasek acquired stakes in Olam International, a local company involved in supply chain management in the agricultural products field.[45]

In early 2009, Temasek increased its stake in Neptune Orient Lines (NOL) through a rights issue. Temasek had held stakes in NOL since 1975. As of end of March 2009, Temasek held about a 67 percent stake in NOL. Earlier, in September 2008, NOL pursued a plan to take over the German container shipping company Hapag–Lloyd, which could have made NOL the third largest container carrier worldwide.[46] The proposal caused uproar among shipping workers in Germany and NOL dropped the deal. Other major investments by Temasek include a S$150 million stake in Hong Kong–based Lung Ming Investment Holdings, which operates an iron ore mine in Mongolia, a 15.4 percent stake in a Brazilian onshore oil field service company called San Antonio International, and a 19.5 percent stake in ENK, a Korean supplier of compressed natural gas (CNG) cylinders.[47] This shows Temasek pursues a well diversified portfolio (both in terms of industry and geography) with little or no controversy.

Temasek's performance prior to the recent financial crisis and in general during normal economic activity has not been very different. The fund has actively sought ways to increase its net worth and in doing so has used its network of subsidiaries. Of the 35 GLCs that were transferred to Temasek in 1975 at least five companies are still in existence. These include DBS Group Holding (corporate and investment banking) in which Temasek has a 28 percent stake, NOL with a 67 percent stake, Singapore Airlines (SIA) with a 55 percent stake, Keppel Corporation (offshore marine infrastructure) with a 21 percent stake, and Wildlife Reserve Singapore (the parent company of Singapore zoo, Night Safari, and Jurong Bird Park) with an 88 percent stake.

Between 1975 and 2000, at least 12 other GLCs—including MediaCorp (national broadcaster), SingTel (Singapore Telecommunications), and the three power companies discussed earlier—were transferred to Temasek. During 2000 and 2002, Temasek began to expand its portfolio into the real estate sector. It acquired a 40 percent stake in CapitaLand[48] in 2000. In 2001, Temasek established

---

43   "Temasek Review 2009."

44   "Mapletree," http://www.mapletreeindustrial.com/.

45   "Temasek Review 2009."

46   "Singapore's NOL Says Drops out of Race to Buy Hapag–Lloyd," *AFP*, 10 October 2008.

47   "Temasek Review 2009."

48   CapitaLand is the largest publicly listed property group in Southeast Asia. It was established in November 2000 as a result of merger between two local property developers (DBS Land and Pidemco Land).

its fully–owned property unit, i.e., Mapletree Investments. Since 2002, Temasek has gradually shifted its focus from the domestic market and OECD countries to Asia and countries closer to home. As a result, the value of investment in Asia (outside of Singapore)—expressed as a percentage of the total value of Temasek's portfolio—increased from 16 percent in 2004 to 34 percent in 2006, and to 46 percent by March 2010 (see Table 5.1).

Since 2004, Temasek has actively expanded its investment through joint ventures between its portfolio companies and other entities around the globe, and has re–aligned its portfolio with market realities. The main investment arm of Temasek in financial services is Fullerton Financial Holdings (originally called Asia Financial Holdings–AFH). Through Fullerton, Temasek acquired stakes in (and later divested from) Bank Danamon Indonesia, Bank Internasional Indonesia (BII), Minsheng Bank (China), China Construction Bank, Bank of China (BOC), ICICI Bank (India), First India Credit Corporation, Hana Bank (South Korea), Alliance Bank (Malaysia), NIB Bank (Pakistan), E.Sun Financial Holding (Taiwan), and Siam Commercial Bank (Thailand).

Other major investments during 2004 and 2005 included Hopson Development Holdings (a developer of residential properties in China), Mahindra & Mahindra (India's largest manufacturer of utility vehicles as well as the Scorpio SUV) through Temasek's wholly–owned subsidiary Aranda Investments[49], and Apollo Healthstreet (an Indian medical outsourcing company) through Maxwell Mauritius, a wholly–owned subsidiary of Temasek.[50] Investments in Southeast and East Asia included a co–investment with Cargill in oil palm plantation in Indonesia and Papua New Guinea, investments in PT Chandra Asri (Indonesia's largest producer of ethylene), and i–Logistics Corporation (a Japanese logistics firm specializing in international multi–modal distribution services). Temasek's presence in other parts of the world included a partnership with Troika Dialog Asset Management to target markets in Russia and the former Soviet Union, a co–investment with two American private equity firms (Silver Lake Partners and KKR) to form Avago Technologies, which is involved in the semiconductor industry, and a co–investment with Istithmar, the SWF of Dubai, in Thailand's healthcare sector.[51]

Perhaps the only controversial investment by Temasek was the acquisition of a stake in the Thai wireless communication company, Shin Corporation Public, in January 2006. Temasek, through two Thai–registered companies, Cedar Holdings and Aspen Holdings, acquired 49 percent of the company from the family of the then Thai Prime Minister, Thaksin Shinawarta, for $1.9 billion.[52] By late May,

---

49   "Temasek Holdings' Subsidiary Acquires 5.5 Million M&M Shares," (Temasek Holdings, 2005).

50   "Apollo Hospitals Group Company, Apollo Health Street Creates an Industry Landmark," (Temasek Holdings, 2005).

51   "Temasek Review 2006."

52   Vivian Wai-yin Kwok, "Temasek's Profits Receive Kick in the Shin," *Forbes. com*, 2 August 2007.

Cedar and Aspen held a 96 percent stake in Shin Corp through a mandatory offer to shareholders. Aspen is owned directly by a Temasek subsidiary while Cedar is 49 percent owned by Temasek.[53] In Thailand, the transaction stirred up anti–Thaksin feelings, and in particular, the belief that the prime minister "avoided taxes and put an important national asset in the hands of foreigners, namely Singapore's government–run Temasek Holdings."[54] Temasek later reduced its stake in Shin Corp and, as of the end of March 2009, Temasek held only a 42 percent stake.

Since late 2006, the pace of portfolio adjustment (investment or divestment) has slowed down. In late March, Temasek, through Dover Investments—its wholly–owned subsidiary[55]—increased its stake in Standard Chartered Bank to about 19 percent.[56] Later in December, Temasek also acquired about a 15 percent stake in Fraser & Neave Limited through its wholly–owned subsidiary Seletar Investments, which marked its most substantial investment in the food and beverage industry.[57] In early 2007, Temasek also boosted its investment in the technology sector and increased its stake in STATS ChipPac (through its wholly–owned subsidiary Singapore Technologies Semiconductors) from 35 percent to about 83 percent.[58]

During financial year 2009–2010, Temasek divested about S$6 billion of its assets and made about S$10 billion of new investments in various companies such as Niko Resources (Canadian oil and gas company), Inment mining (Canadian copper producer), Platmin Limited (South African Platinum producer), as well as Brazilian, Chilean, South Korean, Chinese, and Indian companies. It also established a wholly–owned global investment company, i.e., SeaTown Holdings, with a starting capital of S$40 billion.[59]

In addition to being an active investor and fund manager, Temasek has also been involved in developmental initiatives and humanitarian efforts. On numerous occasions, Temasek and its portfolio companies have assisted with crisis management and natural disaster relief efforts in neighboring countries. In fact, Temasek's engagement in development and social activities started in 1997 with the Singapore Technologies Endowment Program (STEP). STEP organizes youth programs throughout Asia and has more than 1,200 participants from 13 countries, including ASEAN member states, i.e., China, India, Kazakhstan, and the United Kingdom. Recently, Temasek established two philanthropic organizations, Temasek Trust and Temasek Foundation. The former manages the donations

---

53   "Thai Shin Says Temasek Stake Sale Depends on Market," *Reuters*, 24 August 2009.

54   "Pressure Tells: Temasek Calls for Polls," *Asia Times*, 25 February 2006.

55   "The Tan Sri Khoo Teck Puat Estate Agrees to Sell Shares in Standard Chartered to Temasek," (Temasek Holdings, 2006).

56   "Temasek Review 2008," (Temasek Holdings, 2008).

57   "Temasek Holdings (Private) Limited Announces Investments in Fraser & Neave Limited," (Temasek Holdings, 2006).

58   "Temasek Review 2008."

59   "Temasek Review 2010," 38-9.

received from Temasek and other parties, while the latter identifies developmental opportunities in Asia. Funds donated to the Trust are managed actively by Temasek fund managers. Through this structure, about S$16 million have been allocated to 14 programs in Asian countries, including China, India, the Philippines, Vietnam, and Singapore.[60]

In May 2003, Temasek and six of its portfolio companies came to China's aid in 'its battle against the Severe Acute Respiratory Syndrome (SARS) epidemic by providing 20 ventilators for use in hospitals and two thermal imaging scanners for use by the Civil Aviation Authority of China (CAAC). Ho Ching, the Executive Director at the time, also paid a courtesy call on the Chinese vice prime minister and health minister.[61] Between July and August, Temasek and its portfolio companies provided the same equipment to Taiwan, Indonesia, and Vietnam.[62]

In January 2005, after South Asia was hit by the tsunami, Ho Ching, now the CEO of Temasek, sent a sympathy message to victims and survivors of the disaster, expressing Temasek's commitment to support relief and reconstruction efforts. She maintained: "We have set aside $10 million for relief, recovery and reconstruction support. We have already disbursed or committed $1 million for immediate relief in the first week of the disaster... Apart from funds, we have also leveraged on our network of partnerships with companies, NGOs, governments and private groups to focus on resolving issues such as logistics, water, communications and medical care, to help aid to reach those in need. We will continue to work with partners to support the recovery and reconstruction efforts."[63]

In addition to community building and developmental projects, Temasek has also focused on health and human capital development. In 2001, the Singapore Millennium Foundation (SMF) was established with a focus on research and higher education. More than 200 postgraduate scholarships have been given out in areas such as engineering, physical and material sciences, life sciences, and water and renewable resources. In 2007, SMF awarded S$12.5 million for research in liver cancer, mental health, and bio–diesel fuels. In August 2002, Temasek founded the Temasek Life Sciences Laboratory (TLL), which coordinates the research efforts of a team of scientists from more than 25 countries focusing on molecular biology, genetics, plant and animal sciences, solutions for food supply and safety, healthcare (e.g., the low–cost easy–to–use diagnostic kits for the H5N1 bird flu virus), and renewable bio–resources.[64]

---

60   "Temasek Holdings," www.temasekholdings.com.sg.
61   "Temasek Group of Companies Support China's Battle against SARS," (Temasek Holdings, 2003).
62   "Goodwill Contribution by Temasek Group of Companies to Vietnam," (Temasek Holdings, 2003).
63   "Temasek's Relief Efforts in Asia's Tsunami Disaster," (Temasek Holdings, 2005).
64   "Temasek Holdings."

Responsible Entrepreneurship

Temasek is an interesting case in several respects. First, unlike many other SWFs, which are funded by foreign exchange, Temasek is endowed with a portfolio of companies transferred to it by the Ministry of Finance. Second, Temasek has acted as a vehicle for privatization for the government and was tasked to improve the efficiency of GLCs, making them internationally competitive for the purpose of selling them. This allowed the state to reduce its involvement in the economy while remaining committed to long term economic development and an open economy.

The third feature unique to Temasek is the issuance of bonds. As discussed earlier, between 2005 and 2009 Temasek issued three series of US dollar denominated bonds with a total value of $3.25 billion. This was followed by five series of bonds denominated in Singaporean dollar with maturity of between ten and 30 years. There is no information regarding how and where these funds are exactly being used, but the fact that Temasek raised money on the commercial international market most likely indicates the need for liquidity for daily operations of Temasek and its portfolio companies, and perhaps for new portfolio investment.

Transparency is a feature for which many have praised Temasek. The SWF Institute assigned an M–L Transparency index rating of ten to the fund. Since 2005, Temasek has published annual financial reports. Additionally, Singapore has been a member of the IWG of SWFs, which later became the International Forum of SWFs. Despite its participation in international forums and publishing financial reports, some aspects of Temasek's operations remain unclear. For instance, we do not know much about the operations of the fund during the period between its inception in 1974 and the turn of the century, nor do we exactly know how the investment (or divestment) decisions are made by its management. Nevertheless, no evidence was found showing that Temasek assets or returns were ever used for balance of payments corrections or as a foreign policy tool.

Another interesting aspect of the fund is the nature of the relationship between Temasek's business leaders (board of directors, management, and various advisory boards), the management of the subsidiary and portfolio companies, and the government. A number of board members of Temasek currently serve (or have served) as board members or executives of other companies. Some of them have been government officials. In addition to many years of experience, these board members bring with them an extensive network of government officials and business leaders, which most likely has influenced or facilitated business decisions. Temasek continuously strives to expand and strengthen its relations with a network of business partners, think tanks, and policy makers around the world.

As discussed earlier, the members of the Board of Directors of Temasek are closely connected with the past or present government through holding high level public positions or serving as executives of other government–owned companies. In effect, there is very little, if any, external fund managers and all decisions about investment strategies are made by Temasek management team and directed by the board's guidance. The president's approval is also needed for the appointment or removal of board members. Despite the close connection between Temasek and the Singapore government, government political decisions seemed not to have impacted Temasek's strategy. Changes in the government have virtually no impact on the operations of the fund as Temasek assets and returns are protected by the Constitution since 1991. Temasek assets and returns were excluded from the new arrangements under the two amendments to the Constitution which were introduced in 2001 and 2008 in response to fiscal contraction.

Additionally, there has been no evidence of Temasek making overseas investments in non–commercial or politically sensitive areas. The industries, in which Temasek has invested, range from banks and investment companies to resources, technology, and telecommunications around the world, with almost no political backlash or scrutiny. In the case of the controversial investment in Shin Corporation in Thailand, Temasek preferred the offloading of its investment to political controversy. The government officials in Singapore continuously emphasize the commercial approach of the fund. They also remain sensitive to public opinion with respect to the role of the government in the economy and Temasek's internal affairs. In fact, both the Singapore Ministry of Finance and Temasek have, on various occasions, reacted to major newspapers' op–eds or editorials on topics such as government involvement in the economy, transparency, and the sudden change of course with respect to the appointment of the new non–Singaporean CEO. In May 2000, for instance, two days after a column published in *The Strait Times* (one of the major local newspapers) criticizing the continued government ownership of major companies, Temasek issued a press release defending its position and stressing that its portfolio companies have performed on a commercial basis and that the process of privatization would not be a quick one.[65]

During the months of August and September 2009, both the Ministry of Finance and Temasek responded to *The Wall Street Journal*, defending the fund's position with respect to issues discussed previously in the *Journal*'s opinion section. On the issue of transparency and disclosure, the Ministry of Finance asserted that Temasek "discloses all relevant information that Singaporeans need to judge Temasek's performance as a long–term investor ... Temasek itself discloses well beyond what it is required under the law."[66] Regarding the sudden departure of Goodyear, the Ministry argued that "what Temasek stated about the mutual agreement not to proceed with the planned CEO succession is no different from typical disclosure by large companies ... while it is ideal to have a Singaporean [CEO], this is not always possible, as the field of candidates with experience in running international operations is narrow."[67] Temasek also reacted to another op–ed that had called

65   "Temasek Cannot Divest Stakes in GLCs Overnight," (Temasek Holdings, 2000).

66   Chin Sau Ho, "Singapore, Temasek and Disclosure," *The Wall Street Journal*, 25 August 2009.

67   Ibid.

Temasek "another government appendage,"[68] by stressing that Temasek was "an investment company set up as asset owner to seek returns by taking investment risks."[69]

The Singaporean government involvement in Temasek, and in the economy in general, does not reflect economic statecraft but rather public entrepreneurship that dates back to the creation of Singapore as an independent state. In fact, as early as the 1970s, the government of Singapore realized that smallness and domestic market limitations were impediments to economic development and that efficient management of the SOEs required an entrepreneurial entity outside of the formal political structure. Dr. Goh Keng Swee, the architect of Singapore's modernization believed:

> The role that is to be accorded to private entrepreneurs in the development plans
> of underdeveloped countries not only depends on political attitudes, but to some
> extent is influenced by the adequacy of the supply of entrepreneurs ... The role
> of entrepreneurs, broadly, is to perform the function of risk–taking by investing
> capital in new ventures. They introduce innovations in processes or in products.
> It is on the successful performance of entrepreneurs that continuous economic
> expansion in modern industrial society largely depends.[70]

Since 1965, when Singapore became an independent state, the government has been continuously involved in managing the economy. It established new industries and SOEs to run various economic sectors such as maritime and shipping, power generation, and telecommunications. The government also designed and led the import substitution, and later the export promotion as well as the economic development strategies.

In fact, the level of government involvement in the economy has been so great that, according to some, it has become counterproductive. Lim et al maintained, "[the] state capitalism built by civil servants turned entrepreneurs has added a new dimension to the competition between the public and private sector, in that it has alienated local business groups and to some extent the professional classes."[71] State involvement in the economy in the case of Singapore is undeniable. Nevertheless, the entrepreneurial spirit has become embedded in the management of various industries or state–owned companies, with Temasek being a prominent example.

While the GIC and MAS each respectively manage the official reserves of the country and administer the monetary policy of the economy, Temasek manages the government's stakes in various companies. It is mandated to "create and

---

68   "Temasek's Revised Charter," *The Wall Street Journal*, 31 August 2009.

69   Myrna Thomas, "Correcting Temasek Misperceptions," *The Wall Street Journal*, 8 September 2009.

70   Keng Swee Goh, *The Economics of Modernization and Other Essays* (Singapore: Asia Pacific Press, 1972), 80.

71   Lim, Fong, and Findlay, "Five Small Open Economies," 109.

deliver sustainable long–term value ... increase, reduce, or hold its investments in companies or other assets, or pioneer innovative products or businesses in order to create and maximize shareholder value."[72] As indicated in the 2009 Temasek Review, the fund has "a flexible investment horizon and look[s] to create optionalities for future value,"[73] and it also has "the flexibility of taking concentrated positions or investing with a long or short horizon."[74] Almost the entire portfolio of Temasek consists of stakes in various companies, resulting in a large holding of equities rather than a less liquid position or investment in low risk fixed–income assets.

In fact, Temasek's performance is comparable to private holding companies. As mentioned earlier, when short on cash, Temasek issued bonds like any other commercial entity in order to raise money for its operations and portfolio companies. Additionally, the CEO and Executive Director of Temasek, Ho Ching, indicated that there was a possibility of bringing in co–investors in the long run to ensure the sustainability of the fund's operations. She maintained that Temasek "would seek 'sophisticated co–investors' and would not sell the 'family jewels' for short–term gains."[75] Although many questions—e.g., whether "sophisticated investors" refers only to domestic investors or includes international investors, and if so, whether Temasek would still be considered a SWF or not—remain to be answered, nevertheless, the management's approach indicates the entrepreneurial spirit that guides Temasek today.

The reality is that Singapore is a small country with no significant stock of natural resources. The size of the domestic market is small even after including the regional market. Singapore has always relied heavily on regional and international trade, and this openness has left the country vulnerable to external shocks. Since gaining independence, Singapore has experienced several financial crises. However, the government—or more precisely—the "PAP did not abandon the colonial administration's commitment to free trade, competition, and free enterprises, it felt that the state should ... take the lead in establishing new economic activities, especially in industries where the private sector had neither the experience nor the capital to operate successfully."[76]

Singapore has a well-developed tax system but its tax rates were kept at relatively low levels. In fact "[t]he fundamental tenet of Singapore's tax policy is to keep tax rates competitive both for corporations as well as individuals."[77] The government is committed to a balanced budget and running a deficit is possible only if the incumbent government has already built up reserves during its five–year

---

72   "Temasek Review 2010," 5.
73   "Temasek Review 2009," 37.
74   Ibid., 34.
75   Gwen Robinson, "When Is an SWF Not an SWF?," in *FT Alphaville* (2009).
76   Lim, Fong, and Findlay, "Five Small Open Economies," 107-08.
77   "An Overview of the Singapore Tax System," Inland Revenue Authority of Singapore, http://www.iras.gov.sg/irasHome/page04.aspx?id=5676.

term. Nevertheless, global downturns or unforeseen circumstances may require the government to expand its revenue base. As discussed earlier, the two amendments to the Constitution, which were passed in response to fiscal contractions, allowed the government to draw upon the investment income of its GLCs. However, Temasek was excluded from the 2008 arrangement where the government was allowed to make withdrawals from the long–term expected returns.

Today, Temasek manages a portfolio of companies on behalf of the Singapore government. The government is allowed to withdraw up to half of the returns accumulated within the current government term for budgetary purposes. Beyond this contribution, there is no evidence or indication that Temasek is providing resources to assist the government in coping with international financial imbalances or meeting public pension fund obligations. As mentioned earlier, the government relies more on other sources of domestic compensation including, GIC which manages official reserves and the CPF which is the national pension scheme that manages funds contributed by both employees and employers. Temasek, above all, is the embodiment of the Singapore government's entrepreneurial spirit and seems it will be so at least in the near future.

References

"Apollo Hospitals Group Company, Apollo Health Street Creates an Industry Landmark." Temasek Holdings, 2005.

Bennett, Simon. "Temasek's Mapletree Plans to List S$4 Billion REIT." *Bloomberg*, 12 September 2009.

Blöndal, Jón R. "Budgeting in Singapore." Organisation for Economic Co–operation and Development, 2006.

"Budget Highlights, Financial Year 2009: Keeping Jobs, Building for the Future." Singapore Ministry of Finance, 2009.

Burton, John. "Temasek and US's Goodyear Part Ways." *Financial Times*, 22 July 2009.

Chan, Fiona. "Goodyear Rumors 'Far from the Truth'." *AsiaOne*, 1 August 2009.

"Frequently Asked Questions About Temasek Holdings." Temasek Holdings, http://www.temasekholdings.com.sg/pdf/TemasekHoldingsFAQs.pdf.

Gerschenkron, Alexander, and Seymour Martin Lipset collection. *Economic Backwardness in Historical Perspective, a Book of Essays*. Cambridge, Mass.: Belknap Press of Harvard University Press, 1962.

Goh, Keng Swee. *The Economics of Modernization and Other Essays*. Singapore: Asia Pacific Press, 1972.

"Goodwill Contribution by Temasek Group of Companies to Vietnam." Temasek Holdings, 2003.

Ho, Chin Sau. "Singapore, Temasek and Disclosure." *The Wall Street Journal*, 25 August 2009.

Koh, Tommy T. B., and Li Lin Chang. *The United States-Singapore Free Trade Agreement: Highlights and Insights*. Singapore: World Scientific Pub; Institute of Policy Studies, 2004.

Kwok, Vivian Wai-yin. "Temasek's Profits Receive Kick in the Shin." *Forbes. com*, 2 August 2007.

Lim, Linda, Pang Eng Fong, and Ronald Findlay. "Five Small Open Economies." In *A World Bank Comparative Study. The Political Economy of Poverty, Equity, and Growth.*, edited by Ronald Findlay and Stanislaw Wellisz. New York: Published for the World Bank [by] Oxford University Press, 1993.

Lopez, Ditas. "Temasek Looks to Tap U.S. Bond Markets." *The Wall Street Journal*, 20 October 2009.

"Mapletree." http://www.mapletreeindustrial.com/.

"Merill Posts 3rd–Quarter Loss of $5.2 Billion." *The New York Times*, 16 October 2008.

"An Overview of the Singapore Tax System." Inland Revenue Authority of Singapore, http://www.iras.gov.sg/irasHome/page04.aspx?id=5676.

"Pressure Tells: Temasek Calls for Polls." *Asia Times*, 25 February 2006.

Robinson, Gwen. "When Is an SWF Not an SWF?" In *FT Alphaville*, 2009.

Schmandt, Jurgen, and C. H. Ward. *Sustainable Development: The Challenge of Transition*. Cambridge, U.K.: Cambridge University Press, 2000.

"Second Reading Speech for Constitution of Republic of Singapore (Amendment) Bill 2008." Singapore Ministry of Finance 2008.

"Singapore Temasek to Sell Power Firm PowerSeraya." *Xinhua*, 7 October 2008.

"Singapore: Temasek to Sell Electricity Generator." *Mysinchew.com*, 8 October 2008.

"Singapore's NOL Says Drops out of Race to Buy Hapag–Lloyd." *AFP*, 10 October 2008.

"The Tan Sri Khoo Teck Puat Estate Agrees to Sell Shares in Standard Chartered to Temasek." Temasek Holdings, 2006.

"Temasek and Transparency–II." *The Wall Street Journal*, 21 July 2009.

"Temasek Cannot Divest Stakes in GLCs Overnight." Temasek Holdings, 2000.

"Temasek Group of Companies Support China's Battle against SARS." Temasek Holdings, 2003.

"Temasek Holdings." www.temasekholdings.com.sg.

"Temasek Holdings (Private) Limited Announces Investments in Fraser & Neave Limited." Temasek Holdings, 2006.

"Temasek Holdings' Subsidiary Acquires 5.5 Million M&M Shares." Temasek Holdings, 2005.

"Temasek Review 2006." Temasek Holdings, 2006.

"Temasek Review 2008." Temasek Holdings, 2008.

"Temasek Review 2009." Temasek Holdings, 2009.

"Temasek Review 2010." Temasek Holdings, 2010.

"Temasek's Relief Efforts in Asia's Tsunami Disaster." Temasek Holdings, 2005.

"Temasek's Revised Charter." *The Wall Street Journal*, 31 August 2009.

The Committee on Financial Services, United States House of Representatives. *Testimony by Simon Israel, Temasek Holdings: A Dependable Investor in the United States*, 5 March 2008.

"Thai Shin Says Temasek Stake Sale Depends on Market." *Reuters*, 24 August 2009.

Thomas, Myrna. "Correcting Temasek Misperceptions." *The Wall Street Journal*, 8 September 2009.

Chapter 6
How Russia Exhausted the National Wealth Fund at an Early Age

The fourth case study looks at the National Wealth Fund (NWF) of the Russian Federation. This is an interesting case and indeed a unique opportunity to study a fund in its nascent stage very closely. The NWF, which is often referred to as the Welfare Fund in the media, was established in 2008 as a result of the split in the four–year old Stabilization Fund. The NWF is, in a sense, a continuation of the Stabilization Fund. Therefore we cannot study the history of one without studying the history of the other. The post–1991 events had a significant impact on the thinking of economic policy makers in Russia. The Stabilization Fund was established in 2004 with the aim of sterilizing the windfall of oil revenues and providing resources for correcting fiscal deficit. After 2008, the task of protecting the oil–based economy from the volatility of oil prices was transferred to the Reserve Fund, while the NWF was created to provide resources for government pension obligations or other fiscal needs. As of 1 August 2010, the NWF held about $88.24 billion or 2.66 trillion rubles of assets mostly in the form of currencies. At its peak, the NWF managed about $93.33 billion during November and December 2009.[1]

From a theoretical standpoint, the domestic compensation thesis is most relevant to the case of the NWF today. In fact, the main part of the NWF's assets is held in cash or western government bonds. Another part of the fund's assets was lent to domestic banks or businesses after the recent financial crisis. The Russian fund with its current asset volume, portfolio structure, and management could not be used as a means of economic statecraft. Neither was it capable of serving as an entrepreneurial arm of the state by engaging in sophisticated business deals and maximizing returns. In fact, the entrepreneurship spirit and talent is still missing in Russia in general, and among bureaucrats in particular. More importantly, there has been a continuous domestic power struggle over the access to and use of the NWF resources (and prior to that the Stabilization Fund).

The Stabilization Fund was created during a period of balance of payments surplus and, as its name suggested, was in fact aimed at managing international imbalances. The Stabilization Fund was a success in a sense, as large amounts of Russia's foreign debt (both sovereign and banking sector) were paid off through this fund—some ahead of schedule. As will be discussed, Russia's approach to

---

1   "National Wealth Fund," Ministry of Finance of the Russian Federation, http://www1.minfin.ru/en/nationalwealthfund/.

managing crisis was, in fact, different from other states. The NWF was created during the period when Russia was hit by the global financial crisis. The economic hardship undermined the mandated objective of the fund to the extent that, before the NWF could formalize its investment criteria and asset management, it had to provide some of its assets as domestic loans to banks and businesses or bail out various institutions.

Perhaps the most interesting issue with respect to the NWF is its position within the Russian political apparatus. While the fund is officially managed by the Ministry of Finance, it has been the focus of various centers of power within the Russian government. The constant struggle over access to the fund's resources has also resulted in the fund's inability to develop a solid agenda. As a cautionary note, we need to bear in mind that the NWF is still fairly young compared to other major funds and that the short lifespan of the fund may not allow us to follow the same structure of study used for other funds discussed earlier in this book. The study of a relatively underdeveloped fund has its uniqueness in that many of the challenges faced by the state or the responsible bureaucracy are quite visible. Nevertheless, conclusions about the purpose of the NWF should be drawn in conjunction with the state's priorities.

Russia remains one of the least transparent states in many aspects, including those related to its funds. The Russian fund continues to operate in a non–transparent way, and its management remains closed to external enquiries. Although, the website of the Ministry of Finance has dedicated sections to both the Reserve Fund and the NWF, the publicly–available information is limited only to general literature and chronological aggregate balances of the funds. Similarly, there is little (sometimes inaccurate) information on the actual composition of the NWF assets and whether (or how much of) its assets are held in various forms. Yet information sought through secondary sources including the media as well as comments and observations by people close to the Russian bureaucracy greatly enhance our knowledge about the fund and the politico economic environment within which it has thrived.

From Stabilization to Wealth Fund

The period between the collapse of the Soviet Union in August 1991 and the creation of the Stabilization Fund in January 2004 had a critical influence on the thinking of the economic policy makers in Russia. During this period, the Russian Federation had experienced not only the political and social problems associated with the transition, but also it had to weather a number of economic shocks, for instance in 1994 and 1998. Against this background, the NWF was officially established on 1 February 2008, following the split of the Stabilization Fund into two separate funds, i.e., the Reserve Fund and the NWF. In order to better understand the purpose of the NWF we need to study the Stabilization Fund and look at the economic and political environment prior to its establishment as well as the relationship between the fund and the Russian federal budget.

Between the collapse of the Soviet Union and 1998, high inflation rates and large budget deficits inflicted the Russian economy. On 11 October 1994 or the "Black Tuesday," the exchange rate fell by 27 percent in a single day.[2] A year later, in the summer of 1995, the monetary authorities introduced the currency band that allowed for a moderate and periodic devaluation of the ruble against foreign currencies. Since the mid 1990s, economic policy was characterized by an incongruous combination of tight monetary policy and excessively loose fiscal policy, which resulted in large scale government borrowing—mainly through domestic treasury bills with exceedingly high interest rates, sometimes "lingering 100 percent per annum."[3] Under the pressure of the IMF, the government bonds market was opened to foreign investors, exposing Russia to external markets volatilities.

The Asian financial crisis, which had started in the summer of 1997, reached Russia in late October and resulted in the fall of Russia's stock market by 19 percent from its peak. Almost a year later, the exchange rate came under attack and the creditors started to withdraw their monies on a large scale. As a result, the country's foreign exchange reserves diminished significantly. Russia was forced to both devalue its currency and default on some of its domestic debt. "Inflation that had fallen to the single digits surged to 85 percent for 1998 as a whole. The Russian stock market hit bottom with a staggering fall of 93 percent from its peak in October 1997 ... About half of Russia's commercial banks went bankrupt."[4]

The financial crash of 1998, in a sense, can be attributed to the high exposure of the Russian economy to the global economy, which had resulted from the massive foreign portfolio investment in the country. Anders Åslund, a former economic advisor to the Russian government and currently a senior fellow at the Peterson Institute of International Economics, argued:

> Foreign portfolio investment skyrocketed from a respectable $8.9 billion in 1996 to an incredible $45.6 billion in 1997 or 10 percent of GDP ... At the peak of the stock market in 1997, foreigners might have owned as much as 30 percent of the market capitalization of some $100 billion.[5]

The volatility of the balance of payments account between 1994 and 1998 is also reflected in IMF data on Russia's balance of payments (available only from 1994). As Figure 6.1 shows, the balance of payment account was, for the most part, in

---

2   Anders Åslund, *Russia's Capitalist Revolution: Why Market Reform Succeeded and Democracy Failed* (Washington, D.C.: Peterson Institute for International Economics, 2007), 143.

3   Ibid., 173.

4   Ibid., 179.

5   Ibid., 174.

deficit so long as the average crude oil prices lingered below $20 a barrel, while the excessive borrowing and flight of the private capital worsened the situation. The massive foreign borrowing by Russia also meant that the government had not focused on domestic sources of revenue, i.e., taxes.

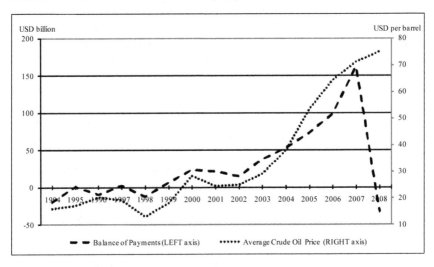

Figure 6.1   Russian Federation balance of payments and oil prices

Source: "International Financial Statistics (IFS)." IMF, 2009.

The turn of the century opened a new chapter in Russia's political economy. The country had fought two wars in Chechnya[6] since the collapse of the Soviet Union; it had undergone political and social turmoil, and was struggling with an out–of–control economy. The economic stabilization began as early as 1999. The government cut expenditures and applied tax laws to large enterprises that had previously enjoyed favorable tax rates. All types of revenue were routed to the federal budget. As a result, the federal budget revenue almost doubled from 11 percent to 20 percent of GDP between 1998 and 2002.[7]

Since the turn of the century, Russia has made progress in joining—and catching up with—the global economic system. In May and June 2002, both the United States and the EU recognized Russia as a market economy.[8] A year later, President

---

6   The first Chechen war took place between December 1994 and August 1996. The second Chechen war started in 1999 but there is no consensus as to when it exactly ended. Some say that it ended in 2002, when the Russia ended its major military operations in Chechnya.

7   Åslund, *Russia's Capitalist Revolution: Why Market Reform Succeeded and Democracy Failed*, 193.

8   Peter Slevin, "U.S. Says Russia Now 'Market Economy'; Designation Follows Announcement by EU," *The Washington Post*, 7 June 2002. Also see "Commission

Vladimir Putin announced that Russia's GDP would be doubled by 2010. In 2005, revenues from the oil and gas sector accounted for 50 percent of the federal budget.[9] The revenues from the oil and gas sector consisted of "hydrocarbon extraction tax (oil and natural gas from all types of hydrocarbon deposits, gas condensate from all types of hydrocarbon deposits); export duty on crude oil; export duty on natural gas; [and] export duty on petroleum products."[10] The Russian government realized that the maintenance of a balanced budget depended, to a large extent, on both the sustainability of revenues (including those from the oil and gas sector) and consistent levels of expenditures.

Against this background and on 1 January 2004, the Stabilization Fund was established. The fund was the brain child of Andrei Illarionov, one of President Putin's maverick economic advisors. The Stabilization Fund, as its name suggested, was designed to sterilize the windfall of oil revenues—by absorbing the excess liquidity and therefore controlling inflation—and providing resources for correcting the fiscal deficit when the price for Urals oil falls below the cut–off price.[11] In practice the role of the fund was two–fold. On the one hand, it accumulated foreign reserves to maintain the stability of exchange rate and domestic prices, and as we shall see, to pay off Russia's sovereign debt. On the other hand, the fund could finance the domestic budget, once it had accumulated a certain level of assets.

The Stabilization Fund was managed by the Russian Ministry of Finance, which set the currency composition and asset allocation, with some asset management functions delegated to the Central Bank of Russia. The fund accumulated assets when the actual price of oil surpassed the cut–off price. Once the balance of the Stabilization Fund exceeded 500 billion rubles, it could release funds to finance the federal budget deficit, pay off foreign debt, or fund other obligations including pension payments.[12]

The fund's assets were to be invested in foreign sovereign debt or foreign currency. The Ministry of Finance could fulfill this responsibility by doing one or both of two things.[13] It could either invest the funds in foreign fixed–income

Recognises Russia as Market Economy," Euroactive.com, http://www.euractiv.com/en/trade/commission-recognises-russia-market-economy/article-115282.

9   "Main Results and Trends of Budget Policy 2008–2010," (Ministry of Finance, Russian Federation).

10   Ibid., 29.

11   The cut–off price is defined in each annual budget according to the Budget Code of the Russian Federation. The cut–off price for 2005 and 2006 budgets were $20 and $27 per barrel respectively. Since 2004, the oil prices have surpassed the cut–off price, bringing windfall of oil revenues to the country.

12   "Stabilization Fund of the Russian Federation," Ministry of Finance of the Russian Federation, http://www.minfin.ru/en/stabfund/.

13   "Procedure for Management of the Assets of the Stabilization Fund of the Russian Federation," in *Regulation of the Government of the Russian Federation No. 229*,

instruments directly,[14] or it could deposit the money in the form of foreign currency in a Federal Treasury account held by the Central Bank of Russia.[15] The second scheme was typically chosen, with a foreign currency allocation of 45 percent US dollars, 45 percent Euros, and 10 percent British pound.

It is not clear how and on what basis the returns were paid by the Central Bank of Russia, nor is it clear whether the Central Bank managed the funds on its own (and paid out the returns after subtracting fees) or managed the funds on behalf of the Stabilization Fund. The Ministry of Finance reported the fund's activities to the government on a quarterly– and annual–basis,[16] and the government passed the same to both Chambers of the Russian parliament (Duma and the Federation Council). The Ministry of Finance has also made the monthly aggregate balance of the fund (in dollar and rubles) available to the public since mid–2006.

Rising oil prices in the period after 2004 (see Figure 6.1) led to a massive accumulation of funds in the Stabilization Fund. A month after its inception, the fund received more than 106 billion rubles from the federal budget surplus. By the end of May 2004, the fund had a balance of 199 billion rubles after it had paid out 333 million rubles for budgetary purposes. By the end of the year, the balance had increased to 522 billion rubles.[17] In January 2005, the Stabilization Fund was able to repay the IMF and the members of the Paris Club[18] a portion of the country's foreign debt, some ahead of schedule. [19] It also paid out 30 billion

---

Government of the Russian Federation (21 April 2006). Quoted in "Stabilization Fund of the Russian Federation."

14   There are certain criteria for the fixed–income instruments. The instruments should be denominated in US dollar, British pound or Euro. Additionally, the issuer has to have the highest credit rating from at least two of the credit rating agencies. The countries whose sovereign debt instrument could be purchased included Austria, Belgium, Finland, France, Germany, Greece, Ireland, Italy, Luxembourg, Netherlands, Portugal, Spain, the United Kingdom, and the United States. For more details see: "Stabilization Fund of the Russian Federation."

15   The returns were paid based on the indices composed if eligible foreign debt instruments, defined by the Ministry of Finance. For further details see: Ibid.

16   "Procedure for Management of the Assets of the Stabilization Fund of the Russian Federation." Quoted in "Stabilization Fund of the Russian Federation."

17   "Stabilization Fund of the Russian Federation: Funds Flow on the Federal Treasury's Account in the Bank of Russian in Rubles in 2004," Ministry of Finance of the Russian Federation, http://www.minfin.ru/common/img/uploaded/library/no_date/2007/rub2004_eng.pdf.

18   The Paris Club was established in 1956 as a lending scheme and provides debt treatment facilities. Currently, the club has 19 permanent and 13 associate members. Russia joined the Paris Club as a permanent member in 1997. The Finance Ministry of Germany is the Russia's main creditor in the club. See "Early Paris Club Debt Repayment to Save Russia $7.7 Bln–Kudrin," *RIA Novosti*, 21 June 2006.

19   The payments included early debt repayment to the IMF (93.5 billion rubles or about $3.33 billion), first debt repayment installment to the members of the Paris Club (430.1 billion rubles or about $15 billion), and servicing the state foreign debt of 1998–

rubles (about $1.04 billion) to the pension fund to finance the state's upcoming pension obligations.[20] Russia made further payments towards its debt in 2006, ahead of maturity. Russian finance minister, Alexei Kudrin, maintained that he was "in favor of making more effective use of Russia's available resources,"[21] and that by making early debt repayments the country would save billions of dollars on fees and interest. In June 2006, Russia paid the last $23.7 billion of its debt and completely discharged its obligations to the Paris Club.[22]

Russia imposed further fiscal discipline and a tight monetary policy. In 2006, currency controls were lifted, the ruble became fully convertible, and the inflation rate was reduced to 9 percent. Still in 2006, there was a great deal of debate over the management of the fund. Kudrin argued that a major portion of the Stabilization Fund should "be invested in foreign government bonds and the rest in large foreign companies."[23] This required an amendment to the Budget Code to allow investment in foreign stocks. Most of the debates centered on the scope of investments and a possible hire of external fund managers. Some argued that this task should be delegated to the Central Bank. In addition to the currency deposits with the Central Bank, it is believed that a portion of the fund was invested in conservative foreign securities such as United States treasury bills until February 2008.[24] The Stabilization Fund, as a result, remained a precautionary reserve and efforts to open its portfolio to riskier assets remained futile. The fund's management, at this stage, was nowhere near being a profit–maximizing entrepreneur.

The Stabilization Fund was a subject of heated debates and a great deal of political contention in 2007. Various rent–seeking groups had an eye for the fund's resources, while President Putin was pushing for more public expenditures to be funded by the Stabilization Fund. During his last year as president, Putin pressed for distribution of billions of rubles of the fund's assets to three government agencies, i.e., the Development Bank, the Investment Fund, and the Russian Venture Company, which in return were supposed to fund developmental projects such as power stations, roads, and waterways.[25] Putin also urged the government to invest some of the Stabilization Fund in domestic stock market to prop up blue chip stocks such as those of Gazprom and Rosneft. Kudrin was, however, of the

---

1999 (123.8 billion rubles or about $4.3 billion). Source: "Stabilization Fund of the Russian Federation."

20   "Russia's Pension Fund Takes out $1.04bln from Stabilization Fund," *RIA Novosti*, 27 December 2005.

21   "Early Paris Club Debt Repayment to Save Russia $7.7 Bln–Kudrin."

22   "Budget Reform."

23   Kirill Gusev, "Russian Stabilization Fund to Be Invested Abroad," *RIA Novosti*, 13 April 2006.

24   "Oil Fund Manager Warns on Spending," *The Moscow Times*, 19 December 2007.

25   Anatoly Medetsky, "Billions Pledged for Roads, Homes," *The Moscow Times*, 27 April 2007.

opposite opinion. He rejected the president's suggestions saying: "I see no threat to our blue chips, the government's investment only boosts speculative growth."[26]

In fact, many supported Kudrin's point of view. The chairman of the investment bank Troika Dialog, Ruben Vardanyan, agreed with the minister of finance saying that an influx of cash from the state would "overheat" the stock market.[27] Pyotr Kazakevich, the official in charge of the Stabilization Fund, warned that "irrational" spending could fuel inflation and make the economy more dependent on the global oil market. Illarionov, now a senior fellow at the Washington–based Cato Institute and a critic of the Kremlin, admitted that the fund was diverging from its original purpose of absorbing excess liquidity and protecting the economy against oil price volatility. He maintained that a "stabilization fund by definition cannot be used and cannot be spent inside the country."[28]

In practice there was an ongoing struggle over access to the Stabilization Fund assets in the Kremlin, with the *siloviki*[29] or the Kremlin clan fighting for more resources at their disposal, while Kudrin was persisting on his position of withholding the fund's assets. Some state–owned corporations such as Russian Technologies proposed that the Stabilization Fund should provide loans to domestic companies. The Federation Council's Budget Committee demanded that the funds be invested in state–owned companies' bonds or Russian companies' equities.[30] The Kremlin clan is also said to have arranged for the arrest of Kudrin's deputy, Sergei Storchak—who was responsible for the management of the Stabilization Fund at the ministry level— in order to pressure the Ministry of Finance to back down from its position.[31]

Amid these power struggles, Putin announced plans for the split of the Stabilization Fund into two separate funds, i.e., the Reserve Fund and the National Welfare (or Wealth) Fund (NWF) in 2008.[32] While the Reserve Fund was intended to supply funds for budgetary purposes, the NWF was designed to increase—through the active management of funds—available resources in order to meet state pension obligations, which were expected to run a deficit as early as 2012. Between August 2006 and the end of January 2008, the balance of the Stabilization Fund almost doubled. According to the official data, the aggregate balance of the Stabilization Fund was 3,851.8 billion rubles ($157.38 billion) as of the end of January 2008.[33]

---

26   "Kudrin Sees No Threat to Blue Chips," *The Moscow Times*, 23 May 2007.

27   Ibid.

28   "Oil Fund Manager Warns on Spending."

29   Siloviki means "people of the force" and refers to those coming from the Russian military, law enforcement or security services. The siloviki members entered the cabinets of Yeltsin and Putin, and remain powerful elements in the Russian politics.

30   "Oil Fund Manager Warns on Spending."

31   Ibid.

32   The National Wealth Fund was initially to be called the Fund for Future Generations. Later it was referred to as the National Welfare Fund. The official website of the Ministry of Finance refers to the fund as the National Wealth Fund, yet many reporters and analysts still refer to the fund as Welfare Fund.

33   "Ministry of Finance of the Russian Federation," http://www1.minfin.ru/en/.

According to Kazakevich, who was in charge of the Stabilization Fund, the average annual return on fund's assets was 11 percent.[34] On 1 February 2008, as global markets were still plunging, the split of the Stabilization Fund went through.

The new Reserve Fund was similar to the Stabilization Fund but differed from it in that it accumulated not only oil revenues but also revenues from the production and export of natural gas. The size of the Reserve Fund was set to 10 percent of the forecasted GDP each year.[35] The government also introduced concepts and measures for the better management of the fiscal budget. According to a budget study, the key objectives of the proper budget management was maintaining a "stable rate of government spending and private consumption in the long range, and averting fluctuations of macroeconomic indicators, such as inflation, currency exchange rate, amount of federal debt and interests rates on financial markets."[36]

In a move similar to that of the Norwegian government with respect to the budget, the Russian government introduced the new concept of "oil and gas deficit," which reflected the "difference between federal revenues without oil and gas revenues and the amount with oil and gas revenues factored in."[37] In 2008, the fiscal deficit was financed by the oil and gas revenues (including those held by the Reserve Fund) with a maximum amount equal to 6.1 percent of the forecasted GDP. Subsequently, the government set the limits for transfer of oil and gas revenues to the budget. The ceiling was set at 5.5 percent and 4.5 percent of GDP for 2009 and 2010, respectively. In an attempt to lower reliance on revenues from the oil and gas sector, the government set the maximum limit of oil and gas revenue transfers at 3.7 percent of the GDP for subsequent years.[38] This meant a greater share of oil and gas revenues could be directed to the Reserve Fund, and down the road, to the NWF.

On 1 February 2008, the NWF was endowed with an aggregate portfolio valued at 783 billion rubles ($32 billion), held in a Treasury account at the Central Bank. In October 2008, some of these deposits were transferred to Vnesheconombank (the state–owned Bank of Development and Foreign Economic Activity).[39] The NWF's starting portfolio consisted of foreign currencies which included $10.4 billion, €12.7 billion, £1.4 billion, and 7.2 billion rubles. The NWF's mission was defined as a means to "support pension system of the Russian Federation to guarantee long–term sound functioning of the system. Fund's [primary] assignments are to co–finance voluntary pension savings of Russian citizens and to balance budget of Pension Fund of the Russian Federation."[40]

---

34   "Oil Fund Manager Warns on Spending."

35   "Reserve Fund," Ministry of Finance of the Russian Federation, http://www1. minfin.ru/en/reservefund/.

36   "Budget Reform," 29.

37   Ibid., 30.

38   Ibid.

39   "National Wealth Fund."

40   Ibid.

The NWF is third in line when it comes to receiving oil and gas revenues. With the changes in the budget process with respect to oil and gas revenues, the NWF receives funds only if the Reserve Fund has first reached 10 percent of the forecasted GDP.[41] The Reserve Fund receives money only after a certain level of oil and gas revenues has been allocated to the federal budget.[42] The Ministry of Finance is the manager of the NWF and the Central Bank acts as the operational manager. By law, the fund remains open to engaging an external fund manager although the terms of engagement have yet to be drafted.

According to the official website of the NWF, the Ministry of Finance reports the value of the fund's assets, the inflows and outflows, and the allocation of assets each month to the government, which subsequently reports the same to both Chambers of the Russian parliament (Duma and the Council of Federation).[43] The Ministry of Finance claims that audits of the fund are conducted by Russian official agencies and that the Accounts Chamber examines the management, accumulation, and expenditures of the NWF on a quarterly basis. Nevertheless, details of the audits and their results remain internal and not available to the public.

The Russian government has defined the limits within which the Ministry of Finance can establish the NWF's portfolio. Table 6.1 summarizes these limits on the various classes of financial assets that the fund may include. It is, however, not clear how the government determines the criteria. Additionally, the government establishes the criteria determining the eligibility of debt securities. Only the debt instruments of certain states—i.e., Austria, Belgium, Canada, Denmark, Finland, France, Germany, Ireland, Luxembourg, the Netherlands, Spain, Sweden, the United Kingdom, and the United States—can be included in the portfolio of the NWF. Additionally, the debt instruments must comply with certain criteria with respect to the credit rating of the issuing agency. The foreign issuers must have a long–term credit rating of at least AA– (Fitch and S&P rating) or Aa3 (Moody's rating). The instruments should also have a fixed face value and be denominated in approved currencies, have fixed coupon rate and fixed maturity date, and have no call or put options.[44]

---

41   "Budget Code of the Russian Federation," in *Chapter 13.2, Article 96.10, Clause 3*. Quoted in "National Wealth Fund."

42   The government has gradually reduced the amount of distribution of oil and gas revenues to the federal budget. The size of allowable contributions has reduced from 6.1 percent of the forecasted the GDP in 2008 to 5.5 percent in 2009 and 4.5 percent in 2010. In 2008, the required level was achieved at the oil price of $70 per barrel. From 2011 and onwards, the government has limited the use of the oil and gas revenue in the federal budget to 3.7 percent of the forecasted GDP.

43   "National Wealth Fund."

44   Ibid.

Table 6.1   **NWF's investment criteria set by the Russian government (percent)**

Debt securities of foreign states	00–100
Debt securities of foreign state agencies and central banks	0–30
Supranational agencies debt securities *	0–15
Deposits in banks, depository institutions and Vnesheconombank †	0–40
Deposits in the Bank of Russia	00–100
Debt securities of legal entities	0–30
Equities of legal entities and shares of investment funds ‡	0–50

Source: "National Wealth Fund." Ministry of Finance of the Russian Federation, http://www1.minfin.ru/en/nationalwealthfund/.

* Supranational agencies include, Asian Development Bank (ADB), Council of Europe Development Bank (CEB), European Bank for Reconstruction and Development (EBRD), European Investment Bank (EIB), Inter–American Development Bank (IADB), International Bank for Reconstruction and Development (IBRD), International Finance Corporation (IFC), Nordic Investment Bank (NIB).

† The bank or depository institutions should have a long–term credit rating similar to issuers of debt instruments. In the case of Vnesheconombank, maximum deposit amount is set at 655 billion rubles.

‡ Equities must be listed on one exchange market with the foreign equities be included in MSCI World Index and FTSE All–World Index.

Some speculate that $48 billion of the fund assets were invested in foreign bonds, including those issued by government–related agencies in the United States and the United Kingdom, although details about the holdings are not disclosed.[45] As can be seen in Table 6.1, the portfolio can only consist of up to 50 percent equities. The criteria also permit the entire portfolio to be invested in debt instruments or in cash held with the central bank. As can be seen, the overall criteria favors low–risk or risk–free holdings. This portfolio structure also indicates that wealth maximization is not the immediate goal of the fund.

Additionally, the Ministry of Finance can establish its own criteria or requirements within the limits imposed by the government. According to the Ministry of Finance, up to 40 percent of the fund's assets may be denominated in rubles, whereas holdings of foreign currency may constitute up to 100 percent of the fund's assets, in which case the structure of foreign exchange holdings will be 45 percent US dollars, 45 percent Euros, and 10 percent British pounds.[46] Regarding the holdings of debt instruments, the Ministry of Finance has also set the maturity criteria, i.e., for instruments denominated in US dollars and Euros between three months and three years, and for those denominated in British pounds between

---

45   Courtney Weaver, "State Will Start Buying Shares This Week," *The Moscow Times*, 20 October 2008.

46   "National Wealth Fund."

three months and five years.[47] The selection of these foreign entities is still subject to the approval of the Central Bank of Russia.[48] A key point is that the debt holding of any one issue cannot exceed five percent of the aggregate value of that issue.[49] In October 2008, in response to the financial crisis, the Duma decided to place about $17 billion of the NWF assets on deposit with the Vnesheconombank, which would then lend the money to other banks and businesses, including $1 billion to an agriculture bank called Rosselkhozbank.[50] Vnesheconombank also acted as the government broker for the funneling of 410 billion rubles in lending to other banks[51] and injecting of a further 175 billion rubles ($6.8 billion) into the domestic stock market.[52] The bank's chief, Vladimir Dmitriyev, explained that the aim of the move was to diversify fund reserves, make additional investments in Russian stock market, and to refinance the external debts of several companies in the mining and manufacturing sectors.[53]

The S&P had previously criticized Kudrin's plans for using the NWF to support financial markets. In response, Kudrin maintained: "[o]ur participation in the market will have a completely different goal ... [it] will have some healing effect. Maybe we will have to wait three to five years for the assets to grow, but that's okay."[54] According to Anna Zadornova, a Goldman Sachs analyst, the Ministry of Finance had to temporarily "scale back or even abandon its plans to invest (Russia's) oil and gas revenue outside the country."[55]

By the end of November 2009, more than 65 percent of the NWF deposits at Vnesheconombank had been lent to other banks, with about 29 percent of the deposits used to support the Russian stock exchange and the remaining amount lent to small– to medium–size companies. The structure of deposits and their related terms and conditions are established by the Ministry of Finance. Table 6.2

---

47   Ibid.

48   "Order of the Ministry of Finance No. 22, Dated January 24, 2008," (Ministry of Finance of the Russian Federation). Quoted in "National Wealth Fund."

49   "Order of the Ministry of Finance No. 23, Dated January 24, 2008," (Ministry of Finance of the Russian Federation). Quoted in "National Wealth Fund."

50   Andrew E. Kramer, "Russia Approves Loan Plan to Ease Credit Crunch," *The New York Times*, 10 October 2008.

51   "Federal Law No.173–Fz, Dated October 13, 2008 'Additional Measures to Support Financial System of the Russian Federation,' Article 4," (Ministry of Finance of the Russina Federation, 2008). Quoted in "National Wealth Fund."

52   "National Wealth Fund."

53   "Vnesheconombank to Bail out Companies This Week ", *RosBusinessOnsulting (RBC)*, 21 October 2008.

54   Anatoly Medetsky, "Kudrin Says Pension Fund Next up for Stocks," *The Moscow Times*, 13 October 2008.

55   Gleb Bryanski, "Russia Says No Change to SWF Strategy Despite Crisis," *Reuters*, 3 October 2008.

shows the lending limits, the actual deposits level, and the interest rates earned on the NWF deposits as of 1 December 2009.[56]

Table 6.2   Structure of the NWF's deposits at Vnesheconombank (billion rubles)

Eligible Allocation (as of 1 December 2009)	Maximum Allowed	Actual Amount	Maturity	Interest rate (percent)
Loans to Russian banks	410.00	284.34	31 Dec 2019	7.0
		103.45	21 Dec 2020	8.5
Russian stock exchange	175.00	175.00	21 Oct 2013	7.0
Loans to small to medium–size companies	030.00	020.00	25 Dec 2017	8.5
Loans to the Agency for Housing Mortgage Lending	040.00	000.00		
Total	655.00	582.79		

Source: "National Wealth Fund." Ministry of Finance of the Russian Federation, http://www1.minfin.ru/en/nationalwealthfund/.

The NWF deposits at Vnesheconombank and other deposit institutions including the Central Bank earn interest. Interest on deposits with Vnesheconombank is, for the most part, paid quarterly. The Central Bank also pays interest on the funds. The rates are said to be based on the indices approved by the government, although very little is known about the criteria and basis for the rate and the deciding authority.

The aggregate value of the NWF assets has exhibited an upward trend over time, rising from $32 billion (783.3 billion ruble) in February 2008 to $92.9 billion (2,769.8 billion ruble) in December 2009.[57] According to the Ministry of Finance, the fund's assets can only be used to "co–finance voluntary pension savings of Russian citizens and to balance budget of Pension Fund of the Russian Federation."[58] Each fiscal year, the federal budget defines the amount to be transferred to the Pension Fund.

The government allocates about 10 percent of its revenues to the payment of pensions. These payments are made through the Pension Fund and direct budget payments.[59] The actual amount paid from the budget to cover the Pension Fund

---

56   "National Wealth Fund."

57   Ibid.

58   Ibid.

59   Pensions to military personnel and their family members are paid directly through the federal budget. The federal budget then transfers funds to the Pension Fund for three items, i.e., base pension, additional provisions or benefits and compensations, and Pension Fund deficit. Source: "Budget Reform."

deficit was 88.2 billion ruble in 2007. In 2010, the required transfer from the federal budget to the Pension Fund was estimated to be about 251.6 billion ruble.[60]

In 2009, efforts concerning hiring an independent or separate fund manager gained pace. The Ministry of Finance—in coordination with other agencies, including the Ministry of Economic Development and the Central Bank—managed to finalize a draft law, which it had initiated in October 2008.[61] The law dealt with the establishment of the Russian Financial Agency (RFA), a new institutions under the government's control. Dmitry Pankin, the deputy finance minister, announced that he expected that the law would go into force in 2010. The primary role of the RFA was to efficiently manage the state's assets and debt obligations. The expected federal budget deficit may, however, shift the focus to fund–raising. Pankin described the top priority as "managing NWF funds and federal budget liquidity."[62] Although the RFA would still be a state–owned agency, it can be seen as a first step towards a separate fund management structure. Of course, depending on internal politics, the fund may either move in the direction of more independent management or fall into the hands of silovikis, Putinists, or rent seekers.

Torn for Domestic Compensation

The NWF is an interesting and, in a sense, a unique case for two main reasons. First, the fund is very young and domestic processes with respect to portfolio structure and fund management remain immature. Second, and perhaps as a result of the first reason, there has been a constant struggle by various centers of power within the Russian government over access to resources of the fund (and its predecessor, i.e., the Stabilization Fund). The Russian government has been divided between the Ministry of Finance headed by Kudrin and the rest of the cabinet. Without an external and independent fund manager, Kudrin has acted as the guardian of Russian national wealth by keeping the fund's assets outside of the domestic politics. In fact, he managed to resist the Putinist policy makers and the cabinet members, whose push for progress was not necessarily based on a long–term vision of sustainable economic growth.

Putin's view about the NWF was clearly different from that of Illarionov or Kudrin, who understood the importance of the long–term and efficient management of national reserves. At one point, Putin even denied that Russia had a sovereign

---

60   Ibid., 10.

61   The draft strategy indicated that up to 50 percent of the NWF could be invested in equities, and a further 30 percent in corporate bonds. The investment universe included both the emerging and the domestic markets. The draft law also had provisions for a separate (even foreign) fund manager. Source: Bryanski, "Russia Says No Change to SWF Strategy Despite Crisis."

62   "Russian Financial Agency Should Commence Business Starting 2010," *Cbonds*, 14 August 2009.

fund.[63] In June 2008, Henry Paulson—the then United States Secretary of the Treasury—travelled to Moscow to discuss trade and investment between the United States and Russia. During this meeting issues including Russia's investment in the United States and the Russian SWF were also discussed. Interestingly, Putin—then the prime minister—assured Paulson that all the Russian investment in the United States was private. In reference to the topic of SWFs, Putin naively told Paulson: "Since we do not have a sovereign wealth fund yet, you are confusing us with someone else … but we are ready to do it, especially if you want us to."[64] Putin's remarks—apart from being a typical politician's response—may have also implied that he believed the NWF existed to provide financial resources to few elites closely connected to the government rather than to serve and support the long–term domestic public obligations (pensions).

The ownership and management structure of the NWF, in its current form, would not exclude future economic statecraft goals. However, the need for short–term liquidity (primarily for domestic purposes, specifically for maintaining high level of public expenditures) does not allow the Russian government to mobilize and use the fund's resources as a means of statecraft. Additionally, the presence of people like Kudrin in the political apparatus would impose a big challenge for those who try to use the fund's resources for political purposes or short–term goals.

In fact, Kudrin was besieged with demands to direct funds towards the public welfare and the military. In early 2006, only two years after the creation of the Stabilization Fund, the cabinet's deputy chief of staff, Mikhail Kopeikin, argued that leaving the fund to accumulate revenues would result in the waste of almost 600 million rubles over three years and that the fund should invest in riskier, high–yield assets. Kudrin denied Kopeikin's request, and at one point even shouted at the deputy chief of staff, arguing that Kopeikin's claim was "completely uninformed," and that he had "cast a shadow over the president and the government."[65] Illarionov, once Putin's economic advisor and now a Kremlin critic, argued: "I don't think they should take this money out at all, regardless of the speed, regardless of the size. The resources of the Stabilization Fund cannot be used first domestically, and second, in the investment of shares."[66]

In January 2008, as oil prices rose above $100 per barrel, Kudrin asserted that "Russia, which channels most of its oil revenues into its Reserve Fund and NWF

---

63   In fact, with no foreign portfolio investment these funds do not meet the SWF criteria. It was said that some of NWF assets were in foreign bonds, although that could not be verified. Nevertheless, there are provisions and guidelines for investment in foreign instruments. That means the NWF is able to make overseas investment.

64   David Lawder and Gleb Bryanski, "Putin–No Sovereign Wealth Fund in Russia Yet," *Reuters*, 30 June 2008.

65   Courtney Weaver, "Crisis Silencing Kudrin's Critics," *The Moscow Times*, 7 November 2008.

66   Ibid.

would refrain from spending any additional income immediately ... we'll have more money ... we will spend it gradually and according to a plan."[67] Later in October 2008, Pankin, deputy finance minister, stated that Russia did not plan to change the investment strategy of its funds in response to market turbulences,[68] while Illarionov believed that the fund was becoming a "victim of the greed of several groups."[69]

In a sense, Kudrin's firm and relatively independent position with regard to the management of the NWF assets has paid off. According to Jonathan Schiffer, Moody's chief sovereign ratings analyst, "Kudrin has played a very lonely but admirable role ... For all the volatility and the depreciation of the ruble, if you didn't have the stabilization fund, the volatility [of ruble] would be multiplied two or three times. Kudrin has been validated."[70] Over time and especially during the recent global financial crisis, the government's attitude has also mellowed. Some say that the views of Kopeikin, Sergei Mironov (the Federation Council Speaker), and Boris Gryzlov (State Duma Speaker) have turned in favor of Kudrin.

Nevertheless, when Kudrin revealed plans to tap into the NWF as part of the economic stimulus package, he faced a challenge on a different front. The State Duma had approved anti–crisis packages worth a total of $86 billion[71] and, as a result, the government had to use all its resources, including those held by the Reserve Fund and the NWF.[72] Kudrin's announcement was followed by S&P downgrading its outlook rating for Russia. Fitch Ratings also estimated that Russia would lose a total of $160 billion by the end of 2009. Fitch and Moody's, however, did not change their ratings at the time.[73] In response, Kudrin stated: "When I defended the oil fund, I always said we can spend it during the crisis. Maybe I was expected to always say that we should not spend the oil fund, but this is wrong."[74] In summary, the Russian funds (the Stabilization Fund and later the NWF) have been more of a subject of domestic political debates than a means of economic statecraft or a foreign policy tool.

Nevertheless, some people have also asserted that NWF funds (channeled through the Vnesheconombank) have been used at the discretion of Prime Minister Putin, who chaired the Vnesheconombank's oversight board. It is said that Putin helped oligarch friends such as Oleg Deripaska, Roman Abramovich, Igor Vyuzin,

67   Anatoly Medetsky, "Oil Takes a Trip Past $100 Plateau," *The Moscow Times*, 9 January 2008.

68   Bryanski, "Russia Says No Change to SWF Strategy Despite Crisis."

69   "Oil Fund Manager Warns on Spending."

70   Weaver, "Crisis Silencing Kudrin's Critics."

71   "Russian Capital Flight at $33 Bln in Aug–Sept.–Finance Minister," *RIA Novosti*, 17 October 2008.

72   This is a similar situation to other SWF discussed in earlier chapters, i.e., at the times of economic hardship, fund's resources are, most of the times, tapped into by the government.

73   Weaver, "Crisis Silencing Kudrin's Critics."

74   Medetsky, "Kudrin Says Pension Fund Next up for Stocks."

and Sergei Bogdanchikov pay their foreign debts. Deripaska received $4.5 billion to pay off RusAl and Norilsk Nickel loans from the Royal Bank of Scotland; Abramovich received $1.8 billion to pay off Evraz' immediate creditors; Vyuzin's Mechel was bailed out with $1.5 billion; and Bogdanchikov's Rosneft received $4.5 million.[75]

Despite the government's influence over the management and use of the NWF assets, there has been no political comment by any policy maker or influential figure indicating that the fund is to serve as a foreign policy tool. In contrast and as discussed earlier, the political debate over the fund's assets centered, for the most part, on how the assets be distributed among various domestic players. Moreover, holdings of mostly cash (both local and foreign currency) and allegedly western government bonds are far from being threatening to any sovereign state.

There are two important factors preventing the NWF's assets from being managed in an entrepreneurial way. First and most importantly, the fund has never had a coherent management. Although the Ministry of Finance is officially the manager of the fund, its management has been overshadowed by other centers of power. Additionally, there is no clear consensus as to the purpose of the fund. Although at the time of its creation, the NWF was mandated to provide long–term support to the Russian pension system, its purpose has been redefined by various parties, most often as an ad hoc source of funding.

Second, entrepreneurship still does not have a visible manifest in Russia and is often times confused with rent seeking behavior, a legacy of the years of communist rule and its command economy. As Åslund argues "massive rent seeking characterized the collapse of the Soviet system and the early post–communist period."[76] Innovation, learning, and adaptation are absent from the fund's management. Although in Russia there is a long history of state involvement in the economy, this involvement was in the form of command (controlled) economy rather than in the form of efficient management of economic sectors or state entrepreneurship or management of a limited number of SOEs. Additionally, there are no signs of independent management for the fund and even the establishment of the Russian Financial Agency (RAF) does not equate professional asset management by external fund managers. And as it seems, so long as the fund management is in the hands of bureaucrats, the portfolio is invested in low–risk assets (cash deposits or bonds).

One thing is certain and that Russia has had a troubled economy along with occasional political turmoil, domestically and in the region. In addition to that, the internal battles between the government and other influential players, such as the oligarchs, have increased in recent years. Russia is exposed to fluctuations in both foreign exchange and oil prices. In 1998, the ruble started to depreciate

75   Boris Nemtsov, "No More Welfare for Russia's Oligarchs," *Radio Free Europe*, 18 February 2009.

76   Åslund, *Russia's Capitalist Revolution: Why Market Reform Succeeded and Democracy Failed*, 3.

against the US dollar, declining from 6 rubles to 10 rubles per US dollar, and continued upward until it became fully floating against foreign currencies in 2006. During 2009, the interbank exchange rate fluctuated between 36.53 rubles and 28.13 rubles against the US dollar.[77]

Russia has also experienced oil price volatility, which was severe during the recent global financial crisis. In 2008 alone, the spot price of Urals crude (Russia's main export) fluctuated between $137.61 (4 July) and $34.81 (26 December) per barrel.[78] Despite opening its economy, domestic non–carbohydrate economy remains under–developed and Russia remains heavily dependent on its oil sector. According to Professor Vladimir Popov at the New Economic School in Moscow, while fewer than one million of Russia's 142 million people work in oil–related industries, they produce about half of the country's GDP.[79]

Although Russia is not a small state, it has very little control over its terms of trade, and therefore, global market fluctuations can have a significant impact on its economy. Russia is also a resource–abundant country but like many other resource–abundant (oil exporting) countries, its domestic economic structure has not developed or diversified. The personal tax system is underdeveloped and the corporate tax remains low, as the rates are determined primarily by narrow political considerations.[80] Having said all this, it should also be noted that Russia is still a state in transition, both politically and economically. Corruption, domestic political turmoil, and occasional foreign economic shocks have made the pace of the transition sluggish. This makes the domestic compensation argument the most relevant framework for explaining the NWF goals.

Political and economic changes are, nevertheless, taking place in the country and Russia's approach to coping with the global financial crisis is not necessarily similar to that of other states. Instead of borrowing, as the United States did, Russia financed its bailout funds through domestic sources, including the Reserve Fund, the NWF, and the national gold and currency reserves held by the Central Bank.[81] During the crisis, the Reserve Fund resources were quickly used up and consequently, the NWF missed the opportunity to accumulate further assets. Additionally, a portion of the NWF assets was redistributed domestically, in the form of loans through the Vnesheconombank. In May 2010 the government had

---

77   "Historical Exchnage Rates," (ONDA, 2009).

78   "Weekly Mediterranean (Russia, Urals) Spot Price FOB (Dollars Per Barrel)," (Energy Information Administration, 2009).

79   Catrina Stewart, "From Battered to 'Island of Stability'," *The Moscow Times*, 28 February 2008.

80   One of Putin's radical reforms was his new Tax Code in 2000, which cut all taxes to a flat rate of 13 percent, believing that lower tax rates would make the tax evasion less likely. Source: Ibid.

81   Kramer, "Russia Approves Loan Plan to Ease Credit Crunch."

to withdraw additional $11.97 billion from the NWF to finance the budget deficit and public pension payments.[82]

In summary, the NWF in its current form cannot be deemed an instrument of economic statecraft, nor can it be regarded as a manifestation of state entrepreneurship. Its short lifespan and constant battle between centers of power over access to the fund's assets make it difficult to determine whether the fund will be used within the economic framework of balance of payments smoothing, continue to provide resources in support of the budget or, in accordance with its mandate, provide resources for the management of future pension obligations.

The Russian fund continues to operate in a non–transparent way (a source of concern to the IMF as early as 2004 and prior to the establishment of the Stabilization Fund) and its management remains closed to external enquiries. Martin Gilman, a former IMF representative to Russia, maintained: "The preconditions for the fund's successful operation were unlikely to fit together in the Russian context. There were too many governance and transparency issues for a fund like this to really be effective. In a blunt categorization, Russia was not Norway—Russia was more like Nigeria."[83]

As for the future, the young life of the NWF suggests that things are bound to change and both the structure and management of the fund would have to formalize and mature over time. How long this would take is a question we can only answer once the fund has achieved that stage, perhaps in a decade or so. This can also be complicated as the state's priorities also tend to change over time and so would the priorities and purpose of the NWF. Until then, we may continue to observe the struggle between the internal sources of power over more access to the fund's assets and against those few in government position who believe the NWF should be used for the long–term management of assets and for the greater good of the Russian people.

---

82   "Russia Spends $12bln from Oil Wealth Funds in April," *The Moscow Times*, 5 May 2010.

83   Weaver, "Crisis Silencing Kudrin's Critics."

References

Åslund, Anders. *Russia's Capitalist Revolution: Why Market Reform Succeeded and Democracy Failed*. Washington, D.C.: Peterson Institute for International Economics, 2007.

Bryanski, Gleb. "Russia Says No Change to SWF Strategy Despite Crisis." *Reuters*, 3 October 2008.

"Budget Code of the Russian Federation." In *Chapter 13.2, Article 96.10, Clause 3*.

"Commission Recognises Russia as Market Economy." Euroactive.com, http://www.euractiv.com/en/trade/commission-recognises-russia-market-economy/article-115282.

"Early Paris Club Debt Repayment to Save Russia $7.7 Bln–Kudrin." *RIA Novosti*, 21 June 2006.

"Federal Law No.173–Fz, Dated October 13, 2008 'Additional Measures to Support Financial System of the Russian Federation,' Article 4." Ministry of Finance of the Russina Federation, 2008.

Gusev, Kirill. "Russian Stabilization Fund to Be Invested Abroad." *RIA Novosti*, 13 April 2006.

"Historical Exchnage Rates." ONDA, 2009.

Kramer, Andrew E. "Russia Approves Loan Plan to Ease Credit Crunch." *The New York Times*, 10 October 2008.

"Kudrin Sees No Threat to Blue Chips." *The Moscow Times*, 23 May 2007.

Lawder, David, and Gleb Bryanski. "Putin–No Sovereign Wealth Fund in Russia Yet." *Reuters*, 30 June 2008.

"Main Results and Trends of Budget Policy 2008–2010." Ministry of Finance, Russian Federation.

Medetsky, Anatoly. "Billions Pledged for Roads, Homes." *The Moscow Times*, 27 April 2007.

———. "Kudrin Says Pension Fund Next up for Stocks." *The Moscow Times*, 13 October 2008.

———. "Oil Takes a Trip Past $100 Plateau." *The Moscow Times*, 9 January 2008.

"Ministry of Finance of the Russian Federation." http://www1.minfin.ru/en/.

"National Wealth Fund." Ministry of Finance of the Russian Federation, http://www1.minfin.ru/en/nationalwealthfund/.

Nemtsov, Boris. "No More Welfare for Russia's Oligarchs." *Radio Free Europe*, 18 February 2009.

"Oil Fund Manager Warns on Spending." *The Moscow Times*, 19 December 2007.

"Order of the Ministry of Finance No. 22, Dated January 24, 2008." Ministry of Finance of the Russian Federation.

"Order of the Ministry of Finance No. 23, Dated January 24, 2008." Ministry of Finance of the Russian Federation.

"Procedure for Management of the Assets of the Stabilization Fund of the Russian Federation." In *Regulation of the Government of the Russian Federation No. 229*, 21 April 2006.

"Reserve Fund." Ministry of Finance of the Russian Federation, http://www1.minfin.ru/en/reservefund/.

"Russia Spends $12bln from Oil Wealth Funds in April." *The Moscow Times*, 5 May 2010.

"Russia's Pension Fund Takes out $1.04bln from Stabilization Fund." *RIA Novosti*, 27 December 2005.

"Russian Capital Flight at $33 Bln in Aug–Sept.–Finance Minister." *RIA Novosti*, 17 October 2008.

"Russian Financial Agency Should Commence Business Starting 2010." *Cbonds*, 14 August 2009.

Slevin, Peter. "U.S. Says Russia Now 'Market Economy'; Designation Follows Announcement by EU." *The Washington Post*, 7 June 2002, E.01.

"Stabilization Fund of the Russian Federation." Ministry of Finance of the Russian Federation, http://www.minfin.ru/en/stabfund/.

"Stabilization Fund of the Russian Federation: Funds Flow on the Federal Treasury's Account in the Bank of Russian in Rubles in 2004." Ministry of Finance of the Russian Federation, http://www.minfin.ru/common/img/uploaded/library/no_date/2007/rub2004_eng.pdf.

Stewart, Catrina. "From Battered to 'Island of Stability'." *The Moscow Times*, 28 February 2008.

"Vnesheconombank to Bail out Companies This Week." *RosBusinessOnsulting (RBC)*, 21 October 2008.

Weaver, Courtney. "Crisis Silencing Kudrin's Critics." *The Moscow Times*, 7 November 2008.

———. "State Will Start Buying Shares This Week." *The Moscow Times*, 20 October 2008.

"Weekly Mediterranean (Russia, Urals) Spot Price FOB (Dollars Per Barrel)." Energy Information Administration, 2009.

Chapter 7
Conclusions

Why should we study SWFs after all? Many states in the West have had a variety of concerns regarding the investments of sovereign funds. Although the anxiety on the part of the recipient states has been overshadowed by the recent global financial crisis that started with massive defaults on sub–prime mortgages in the United States, the concern still exists and will surface again once the economic recovery is in motion. The primary concerns are generally around a few major topics: SWFs posing a threat to national security, the risk of protectionism in response to the proliferation of SWF investments, the risk of financial instability due to reckless decisions by SWFs, and lack of international oversight over the performance of these funds.

During 2005 and 2006, the United States' concern was more from a national security perspective while Europe was more concerned with the lack of reciprocity, established standards, and openness on the sovereign funds. Policy makers in the United States, whose view was predominantly influenced by realist theories in international relations, were preoccupied with the idea that some foreign governments' ownership in specific areas might expose the country to power manipulation through economic means. Nevertheless, the potential benefits of capital inflows and the fact that not all SWFs investments are threatening, were overlooked amid widespread political debates. Two specific examples are the plan to take over the management of six sea port facilities by the state–owned Dubai Ports World (DP World) and the purchase of Unocal sought by the China National Offshore Oil Corporation (CNOOC).[1]

In the case of the CNOOC, the intense political opposition in Congress halted the formal process of the review of the offer, which in turn caused the CNOOC to withdraw its offer in August 2005.[2] After the uproar over the CNOOC case subsided, DP World, which had acquired P&O (a British company whose assets included six port facilities in the United States), faced the same kind of political

---

1   Interestingly, national security was not an issue in the 1980s when Japanese companies made major investments in movie studios or the Rockefeller Centre, or when in 2007 APM Terminals, a subsidiary of Danish APM Møller, built its $450 million–575 acre facility in Portsmouth, Virginia. The company was the first container terminal developed by a foreign and private company in the United States. Many newspapers such as Metro or Boston Globe are also owned by European investors, but they did not create any concerns.

2   "CNOOC Withdraws Its Bid for Unocal," *Asia Times*, 4 August 2005, 723.

opposition on Capitol Hill. At the end, DP World agreed to sell the facilities to a US–controlled firm.[3]

German chancellor Angela Merkel, while referring to SWFs as "new and completely unknown elements," expressed her concerns over their investments in her country and proposed drafting an investment law that would allow the government to block takeovers by SWFs or other large state–sponsored investment agencies.[4] President Nicolas Sarkozy's concern about SWFs' investments in Europe was more due to the lack of reciprocity. He demanded that the owner states of SWFs (for instance China) increase their countries' openness to the flow of capital from Europe.[5] In the United Kingdom, the Chancellor of the Exchequer at the time, Alistair Darling, maintained that as long as SWFs do not threaten national security or pursue political goals they should be free to invest as they please.[6] The Swiss National Bank authorities' concerns focused on the financial protectionist policies that any unfavorable actions by the SWFs might trigger. The Swiss demanded investment guidelines and more transparency.[7]

The current book, however, has revealed that the bulk of these concerns— especially those political—is unfounded. At the same time, the narrow conception that SWFs are used only for balance of payments corrections is equally non–justifiable. In fact, all of the SWFs studied here had almost constant balance of payments surplus with only occasional deficits, which were corrected in the next period or two. Therefore, in practice there was no need for a separate pool of assets (sovereign funds) for balance of payments corrections.

Additionally, as discussed, none of the funds—even the Norwegian GPF–Global that had incorporated non–commercial motives into its decision–making—was shown to have pursued politically strategic goals to the extent that the fund managed to exert power directly over another state. The strongest case among the four case studies in support of economic statecraft was the case of the Norwegian fund, but even in that case the fund's investment (or divestment for that matter) was mainly based on socially responsible and ethical principles rather than political motives. Norway has indeed communicated with the target states its preferences through divestment, exercise of ownership rights, or the mobilization of opinion

3   Gary Clyde Hufbauer, Yee Wong, and Ketki Sheth, *US–China Trade Disputes: Rising Tide, Rising Stakes*, Policy Analyses in International Economics 78 (Peterson Institute for International Economics, 2006).

4   Carter Dougherty, "Europe Looks at Controls on State-Owned Investors," *The New York Times*, 13 July 2007, 3.

5   "Sarkozy Attacks Wealth Funds on Eve of Mideast Trip," *Reuters*, 12 January 2008.

6   Sumeet Desai, "Darling Says Sovereign Funds Need to Follow Rules," *Reuters*, 19 October 2007.

7   Sven Egenter, "Sovereign Wealth Funds Need Rules–SNB's Hildebrand," *Reuters*, 18 December 2007.

around universal principles such as human rights. Nevertheless, it has never exerted direct political power over the target state.

Another interesting—and somewhat expected—finding is that the political economy of crisis induces the same kind of reaction by the owner states of SWFs. At times of crisis the economic strength of the home state is of paramount importance. Therefore, governments may use SWFs resources to support the domestic economy when deemed necessary. The times of crisis also provided an opportunity to examine whether SWFs in fact pursue politically strategic goals. The expectation was that—during a recession or market downturn—SWFs with sinister goals would still pursue deals and make investments in areas that were not commercially sound. For instance, as a result of the recent financial crisis, the assets of many large corporations in major industries (e.g., automotives or real estate) suddenly became underpriced.

SWFs could have acquired controlling stakes in those corporations and wait for the economic recovery when they could potentially use their influence and exert power over other major corporations, the entire market, or even the host state. However as we saw, the flow of investment was reversed from the western markets to emerging markets. This behavior supports the argument that SWFs do not have politically strategic motives. Instead, they are concerned with the value of the assets under their management. During times of normal economic activity, however, depending on the political economy of the owner state, SWFs may pursue various goals and hence the need for several political economic perspectives for explaining their performance.

The close examination of a cross section of four SWFs, which were selected based on two major criteria, i.e., perceived objectives and level of transparency, provides a basis for drawing general conclusions about a large array of SWFs— whether new or old, established by an industrial or a developing state, commodity– based or non–commodity–based. A word of caution of course accompanies this generalization. As I have mentioned on a few occasions throughout the book, SWFs' agenda is prone to change over time as the owner state's priorities change. The state priorities also change in response to both domestic and international factors including economic, political, social, and even environmental. This means that SWFs should be studied longitudinally and in conjunction with the political economy of their home states. That being said, we can now discuss all four case studies together in order to broaden our view about the entire group of SWFs and apply the same methodology to other funds.

Four Cases, a Comparative Study

The SWFs of Norway, United Arab Emirates, Singapore, and Russia each represented an interesting and unique case. At the same time, the juxtaposition of these four funds—which were selected systematically and based on two important criteria, i.e., transparency and objectives—helps us better understand the nature and functioning of SWFs while avoiding the overgeneralization of findings, a symptom of most studies on SWFs.

One of the characteristics of the selected funds is that they are at various stages of their lives. The oldest funds in the group belonged to Singapore and the United Arab Emirates. Temasek was established in 1974, only nine years after Singapore declared its independence. ADIA was established in 1976 and only five years after the independence. Norway, on the other hand, first established the Oljefondet (Petroleum Fund) in 1990. The GPF–Global was created later when the Oljefundet was transformed into two separate funds. In the case of Russia, the Oil Stabilization Fund was launched in 2004 and was split into NWF and the Reserve Fund in 2008.

With the exception of ADIA—a stand–alone body within the Abu Dhabi government—ministries of finance (or their equivalents) are the custodians of the funds, while the management of the fund may have been delegated to other entities. In Singapore and the United Arab Emirates, funds are managed by boards of directors constituted of people closely connected to the government. In Norway, the fund is mainly managed by the investment arm of the Norges Bank (the Norwegian Central Bank). In Russia the fund is managed by the Ministry of Finance while its management is being influenced—or better to say, pressured— by various centers of power within the country.

Despite the state's ownership and the government guidelines that must be followed, the management of these funds has shown a certain level of independence, whether stipulated in relevant laws or perceived and exercised by the fund managers. The management of SWFs can also be compared to the management of SOEs. Interestingly, Vernon argues, "[m]anagers of state–owned enterprises commonly try to increase their independence from government apparatus, a tendency variously described as a desire for autonomy or discretion or increased bargaining power."[8]

In the case of Temasek, the board of directors has full control over the operations of the fund and neither the president nor the Ministry of Finance can get involved in the management of the fund. In the case of GPF–Global, Norges Bank has to follow the benchmark portfolio set by the Ministry of Finance, but it has a small margin within which it can manage the portfolio freely. In the case of the NWF of Russia, the quasi independence is in fact a result of a power struggle between various centers of influence and authority on the one hand and the minister of finance on the other. As regards ADIA, all investments have to be approved by the board of directors, who also hold various government posts.

The SWFs of Norway, United Arab Emirates, and Singapore all have diverse portfolios, both in terms of type of instruments and geographical distribution of assets. In Norway, 40 percent of the portfolio has traditionally consisted of

---

8   Raymond Vernon, *Exploring the Global Economy: Emerging Issues in Trade and Investment* (Cambridge, Mass. and Lanham, Md: Center for International Affairs, University Press of America, 1985), 204-05.

equities. Since 2007, the allocation of equities has been gradually increased to 60 percent. Although there is no detailed information about ADIA's portfolio structure, various reports indicate that approximately 75 to 80 percent of its portfolio is made up of non–fixed–income instruments. Temasek's portfolio consists entirely of corporate equities. The composition of Russia's NWF portfolio is different from all other funds studied here in that it mainly consists of highly liquid assets (mainly foreign exchange), deposited with either the central bank or the state–owned Vnesheconombank. A small portion of the assets are also said to be held in western bonds.

In terms of the market value, GPF–Global (valued at approximately \$441 billion as of the end of March 2010) and ADIA (with an estimated value of between \$400 billion and \$875 billion before the recent global financial crisis) remain the two largest funds.[9] The market value of assets under the management of Temasek was about \$132 billion as of the end of March 2009. The aggregate balance of the NWF at the end of December 2009 was about \$93 billion but fell to around \$88 billion in August 2010.

With the exception of Temasek, all SWFs examined in this research were established when both the balance of payments and the country's current account were in surplus. The external account framework, as discussed earlier, does not apply to Temasek as it was initially endowed with a portfolio of state–owned companies instead of the liquid assets derived from external accounts, and specifically from the export of the country's abundant resources.

As was discussed, the idea that SWFs were created—as some argue—for balance of payments corrections was not applicable to the selected case studies. After all, many of the funds were created as a result of constant surpluses in the trade balance or the overall balance of payment. Since the inception of Norway's Oljefondet in 1990, the country has had, for the most part, a constant balance of trade surplus with the exception of a few years in later 1980s when the current account balance experienced deficit. In Russia, both the balance of payments and balance of trade have been in surplus since the creation of the Stabilization Fund in 2004. The balance of trade of the United Arab Emirates has also been in surplus since the creation of the fund. Additionally, none of these funds were intended to provide, or did actually provide, resources for balance of payments corrections.

Instead of balance of payments corrections, most of the funds studied here were found to have provided resources for budgetary purpose when needed. In fact, with the exception of Temasek, all funds were used either systematically or on an ad hoc basis (for instance when the country was hit by the global financial crisis) to support the national budget. In Norway, the economic stimulus package introduced in 2009 required the government to withdraw from GPF–Global about 14 times more than it withdrew in the previous year. The United Arab Emirates has included the return on ADIA's assets as a revenue item in the federal budget

---

9   There is no official data on the size of ADIA. Therefore it is not possible to determine which of the GPF–Global or ADIA is the world's largest sovereign fund.

for many years. Most likely, in the face of the recent global financial crisis, more resources were withdrawn from the fund to support the economy of the United Arab Emirates, although the exact information is not available.

The story is a bit different in Singapore as running a budget deficit was not allowed unless the incumbent government has already built up surpluses during its own five–year term. Drawing on past reserves is considered unconstitutional, except in the event of extreme need, in which case the approval of both the President and the Parliament is required. Only recently, the Singaporean government passed amendments to the Constitution which allowed the withdrawal of up to 50 percent of dividends from companies managed by Temasek. The Russian Federation on the other hand, has relied on both the Reserve Fund and the NWF (and their predecessor, the Stabilization Fund) for budgetary purposes as soon as the government has encountered shortage. The NWF assets were even used indirectly to bail out domestic banks and companies last year. The findings from the four case studies are summarized in Table 7.1.

Table 7.1   Various theoretical explanations for creation of SWFs

SWF	BOP Correction	Political Economy Perspectives		
		Economic Statecraft	State Entrepreneurship	Domestic Compensation
GPF–Global, Norway *	n/a	✓		
ADIA, UAE	n/a		✓	✓
Temasek, Singapore	n/a		✓	
NWF, Russia	n/a			✓

* As discussed, the type of economic statecraft that Norway pursues through its fund is different from the traditional realists' view of economic statecraft. Norway's conduct of foreign policy through GPF–Global is benign in a sense it does not exert direct political power over the target state.

The task of evaluating various sovereign funds is anything but simple, but a good methodology based on international political economic theories can facilitate that task. As discussed earlier in this book, a fund's agenda can develop over time. In addition to that, a fund can pursue multiple goals at any point in time. The multiplicity of goals at any point in time and variations in the fund's agenda over time can complicate our investigations. The key in the study of a SWF is to view it within the greater framework of the national system of political economy. We have to first identify the owner state's priorities and then determine the most important goal of the fund at any point in time. As Table 7.1 shows, none of the states studied here used their sovereign fund for correcting their balance of payments. Instead, the performance of each fund was found to be in line with various theoretical political economic perspectives discussed earlier in this book.[10]

Norway's GPF–Global—one of the world's largest funds with the highest transparency index—makes investment decisions that are based on a set of non–commercial principles which are closely aligned with the Norwegian foreign policy. GPF–Global pursues a combination of goals—maintaining a balance between the goal of profitability and making socially responsible investments. As discussed in Chapter 3, Norway has diverged from the goal of being purely commercially–oriented. It has used the fund to passively impose sanctions on companies whose operations are in contradiction to the Ethical Guidelines. Although there is no evidence showing that the fund's financial leverage was applied at a national level and directly over another state, it does not change the fact that the management of the fund can still be influenced by the state's politics.

ADIA, on the other hand, has stayed relatively free of the Emirate's politics and has functioned as a fund manager—seeking (not always successfully) high returns—while providing sources of income for the federal budget. In the absence of reliable information, however, determining which of these goals takes precedence over the other is very difficult. Nevertheless, ADIA seems—at least in the short run—to be more concerned about the diversity of its portfolio, both in terms of geography and type of investment, rather than providing a regular source of income for budgetary purposes.

The cases of Temasek and the NWF show less complexity. Temasek is mainly the entrepreneurial arm of the state. It has acted in the capacity of a vehicle for privatization of the state–owned companies that were not internationally competitive. The government has also been barred by law from withdrawing funds from Temasek for budgetary purposes or for any public expenditure, except for a portion of its returns. Temasek portfolio does not consist of cash or fixed–income instruments. The fund has invested the proceeds from its operations in new or existing businesses, in the region and around the world. The management of Temasek and its investment decision making process follow sophisticated business models. The volume of business deals and the manner in which transactions are conducted—such as the extensive use of network of subsidiaries, formation of business partnerships, and mergers and acquisitions—clearly show the entrepreneurial skills and spirit embedded in its management philosophy, particularly given the absence of a large private sector.

On the other hand, Russia's NWF has been a vehicle for domestic compensation over its short life span. Although the fund was mandated to provide resources for national pension payments, nevertheless, the internal political struggle—especially during the recent global financial crisis—impacted the fund. The fund's assets which were held mostly in form of cash or foreign currency were distributed

---

10   See Chapter 2 for a detailed discussion on various theoretical perspectives that can help explaining the creation and functioning of SWFs.

among major companies or financial institutions. In a sense, the NWF was torn between various centers of power and distributed among oligarchs and silovikis.

What All That Means

There are a number of interesting and important conclusions we can draw based on the findings summarized in Table 7.1. First, each SWF is in some way unique. The structure and nature of the SWFs are based on—to borrow Gilpin's term—the state's national system of political economy. As I have emphasized at the beginning of the book, my purpose was not to select a single theoretical perspective that would be used as the only framework for explaining the behavior of SWFs. A single theory or paradigm is neither sufficient nor appropriate since the funds were shown to be theoretically progressive, meaning that the theoretical perspectives explaining their behavior varied, according to the circumstances. The assertion that SWFs are theoretically progressive is related to each individual fund. On a larger scale and when looking at SWFs collectively, we also observed a divergence among funds with respect to their goals at any point in time. The interesting finding was, however, that there is one condition under which SWFs tend to show a similar behavior, i.e., economic hardship or financial crisis.

As was shown, both the states and the international environment have changed over time and so has the agenda of SWFs. Therefore, depending on the period of study, certain theoretical framework can explain the behavior of SWFs. One important issue here is that SWFs and their owner states do not change all at the same rate in the same direction. For some SWFs, the process of change has been more rapid and obvious than others. For instance, in the case of the GPF–Global of Norway, we saw that the fund was created against the background of an oil crisis (before Norway became an exporter) and the fear of diminishing oil reserves. Later, as new oil reserves were found and sizable assets were accumulated in the fund, the investment strategy of GPF–Global changed. The fund started to include non–economic factors into its investment decision making and the state asserted its foreign policy preferences through its sovereign fund.

The same argument applies to some extent to the Singaporean fund. The fund originally was used to increase the efficiency and profitability of inefficient government enterprises and to sell them to private sector. In other words, Temasek was initially a privatization vehicle. With the passage of time, the fund has evolved to become a more sophisticated holding company. For ADIA change has come relatively late and at a low speed. For the Russian fund, the change in strategy has not been meaningful as the fund still lacks solid agenda and structure.

Notwithstanding these variations, we may conclude that the purpose of these funds is not balance of payments correction. At times of economic austerity, we hypothesized that the funds would provide the resources needed for domestic budget, maintaining domestic demand and rescuing troubled industries. On the other hand, when states were not financially constrained, the hypothesis was that the SWFs would pursue their main goals, i.e., the reason(s) for which they were initially created. These hypotheses were shown to be true in the cases of the four SWFs examined here.

As a side note, we should be aware that—within the domestic compensation perspective and the various internal politics associated with it—the types of domestic compensation provided by the investor states are not the same. The evidence suggests that the domestic compensation, for the most part, was not of a corrupt nature but was mainly for managing macroeconomic deficiencies and budgetary purposes as well as diversification of the economic base. In the case of ADIA and NWF, for instance, the funds were used to manage fiscal deficits, while for Temasek the diversification of the economy was the immediate purpose of domestic compensation.

Second, the developmental stage of the state—in both economic and political terms—can be a good indicator of the purpose of the fund. The research suggested that the SWFs of states that are both politically and economically advanced and sustainable tend to incorporate non–economic factors in their decision making processes. For instance, in Norway—which is a well–established democracy with a stable open economy and a sustainable balance of payments surplus—the fund's agenda has, over time, become more aligned with the national political consensus and the state's foreign policy. On the other end of the spectrum is the Russian Federation—a state that I like to call "late capitalizer," (after the term "late industrializer" in developmental studies). In Russia, the fund was mainly used for domestic purposes and hence was subject to the influence of domestic politics. In summary, the life cycle of a SWF's agenda is closely related to the national system of political economy.

States such as the United Arab Emirates and Singapore are somewhat in between the two ends of this spectrum. Over the past three decades or so, the United Arab Emirates has had a thriving economy with a stable political system based on what Davidson calls the "neopatrimonial model."[11] Still, the state lacks advanced legal framework for economic activities such as debt restructuring and disclosure. Singapore has also had a relatively stable political system with an advanced framework for commercial activities. However, as a city–state, its domestic market is extremely limited. In these types of states, SWFs can act as entrepreneurs, a role that involves taking higher economic risks—while being conservative with respect to political risks—especially in the areas that lack major private actors.

Third, and consistent with the above conclusions, it is inappropriate to pool all funds together and treat them equally, as most analysts and policy makers do. In fact, SWFs "differ significantly in their level of sophistication and appetite

---

11   Christopher M. Davidson, *The United Arab Emirates: A Study in Survival*, The Middle East in the International System (Boulder, Colo.: Lynne Rienner Publishers, 2005).

for risk, as well as in their style of governance."[12] As discussed earlier, both the international environment and the state's domestic structure (in all its political, economic, social, and cultural aspects) undergo changes over time. This means that a state's priorities shift in response to the new environment, and consequently, so does the fund's agenda. In other words, SWFs are like living creatures that evolve over time. Viewing SWFs—whose owner states are typically not at the same developmental stages—equally can lead to inaccurate generalizations, which in turn can result in wrong decisions or irrelevant policies.

For instance, when a commercially–based fund is deemed political, policy makers in the recipient state can block the entry of the fund into their market. This also deprives the recipient state of new capital inflow that could potentially contribute to the increased economic well–being of the recipient state without imposing any political risks. SWFs could also bail out failing corporations, in which case the recipient state would not need to transfer the burden of the bailout to taxpayers, withdraw funds from official reserves, or resort to external borrowing. On the other hand, if a politically–oriented SWF is treated as a purely commercial fund then conflicts are likely to arise between the recipient state and the owner state of the fund. As a point of reference, none of the existing SWFs has acquired any large stakes in a single state or in any politically sensitive area such as defense industry.[13]

Fourth, the idea that the level of transparency can serve to indicate the real agenda of a SWF is superficial, naïve, and most importantly, logically flawed.[14] As has been shown, Norway's GPF–Global—which is praised as the world's most transparent fund—has incorporated non–economic factors into its investment decision making. In fact, it has imposed investment sanctions on specific industries or states. The fund has also taken sides with respect to political or military conflicts in Palestine and Israel, Burma and Morocco.

The fact is that lack of transparency can be a reflection of factors other than a hidden agenda. Some states still lack established or advanced corporate laws, property laws, disclosure policies, or an internationally accepted legal framework for commercial transactions. The SWFs of those states would, most likely, follow the local norms or culture. A lack of transparency can also be merely a reflection of the local culture. While access to information is considered a right in the West, some countries view this access as a privilege. These cultural differences can

---

12   Benjamin J. Cohen, "Sovereign Wealth Funds and National Security: The Great Tradeoff," *International Affairs* 85, no. 4 (2009): 716.

13   What constitute a "politically sensitive" area is open to a great deal of debate and largely depends on the politician's mindset. Some may argue sectors like media and communications can be politically sensitive because the large stake holders (foreign states) can influence the public's opinion in the host state.

14   This topic is discussed in a separate paper by the author. For more information see Manda Shemirani, "Sovereign Wealth Funds: The False Promise of Transparency," *Infinity Journal* 1, no. 5 (2009).

explain why some funds may be reluctant to disclose information. Conclusions and findings discussed here have important implications for the study of SWFs within the international political economy.

A Few Last Words

First of all, the concerns over the possibility of SWFs serving political purpose or posing a threat to the host states are exaggerated. The fact is that the size of the holdings of these funds in foreign entities is usually small. While, for instance, the Norwegian Storting has allowed up to 10 percent stakes in any single business, the average size of holdings of the GPF–Global was only 6 percent. The recent global financial crisis also provided an opportunity for testing the funds' investment goals. If any of the SWFs had hidden agendas or intended to manipulate market forces, they could have potentially done so by gaining control over key financial institutions in the West during and after the recent financial crisis. They could have taken over troubled financial companies, restructured those companies, and later used them to influence markets or economic sectors. Nevertheless, SWFs not only showed little interest in bailing out the distressed financial institutions, but also shifted their portfolio away from the troubled markets in the West to emerging markets. This move indicates that economic profit is of greater importance than the implementation of politically strategic decisions or economic statecraft.

A quick note on the use of the term "strategic" is needed here. This term literary means, "forming part of a long–term plan or aim to achieve a specific purpose."[15] However, economists and financiers on the one hand, and political analysts and policy makers on the other, tend to diverge in their interpretation of this term. While strategic planning or moves in the business world may refer to timely decisions to ensure the economic profitability of an investment, politicians seem to use this term in its broader meaning in the context of national security. But the fact of the matter is that there is no consensus on what "strategic" means and "what constitutes 'economic security' or how to identify a 'strategic' industry."[16] This may have added to the politicians' concern over the motives of the funds. Again, if funds were used for politically strategic purposes, we would expect them to take over key financial institutions in the West, in order to exert financial power over the recipient states once the crisis was over.

The 2008 financial crisis provided an opportunity for observing possible political strategic takeovers by the investor states. Interestingly, we saw that none of the investor states used their funds for political purposes. In fact, most of the SWFs showed no interest in buying under–priced assets that could potentially

---

15   Catherine Soanes, Sara Hawker, and Julia Elliott, *Paperback Oxford English Dictionary*, 2nd ed. (Oxford; New York: Oxford University Press, 2006).
16   Cohen, "Sovereign Wealth Funds and National Security: The Great Tradeoff," 723.

provide the investor states with strategic influence in financial markets. Instead, they diversified further and diverted their portfolio, shifting investment from the industrial countries to emerging markets. The states acted as cautious entrepreneurs rather than maximizers of political power. In summary, SWFs have not been tools of economic statecraft, but at their worst, they have become objects of contestation amongst rent–seeking domestic actors.

The second important, yet rarely discussed issue with respect to the relationship between the sending and recipient states of sovereign funds is that there are dependencies, and therefore vulnerabilities, that go both ways. While the recipient states have various concerns about foreign investments, the owner states of the SWFs are also exposed to various risks. The SWFs' investment in foreign states is subject to the same risks any multinational company, for instance, is exposed to when making foreign investment. Foreign investment has been always subject to both economic and political risks, including risk of nationalization or expropriation, market crashes, natural disasters, and environmental controversies. A good example is ADIA which incurred massive losses as a result of its investment in Citigroup. For the vast majority of SWFs, US dollar is the unit of account which provides owners states of the funds incentive to welcome international financial stability. ADIA, for instance, has large US dollar holdings which "gives it an incentive to maintain both American financial hegemony and international stability."[17] In addition to these risks, SWFs investments are subject to political scrutiny that can range from the unwelcoming attitudes of a recipient state to legal and legislative barriers to entry.

At the same time, the recipient states' perception of the motives of SWFs has been a source of concern for the owner states. The representatives of a number of SWFs, including those of Norway and Singapore, appeared before various committees of the United States House of Representatives during 2008 and 2009 to talk about the agenda of their funds and clarify any misperceptions. The representative from Abu Dhabi took the lead in the International Working Group (IWG) of the SWFs organized by the IMF to facilitate efforts for compiling a set of principles and practices that would govern the performance of the SWFs. The Singaporean fund also published a number of op–eds in the New York Times and occasionally engaged with the public by providing responses to critics. The extensive work of the IWG (later, the International Forum of SWFs), whose members now include representatives from all four SWFs discussed in this book, indicates the collective efforts on the international level to address the existing concerns, both on the part of the owner and the recipient states of SWFs.

The third point is that SWFs—except for the ownership structure—are not much different from some of the large pension or reserve funds, many of which have existed in western countries for many years. Despite their large size and geographically diverse portfolio, the western pension or reserve funds

---

17   Rawi Abdelal, "Sovereign Wealth in Abu Dhabi," *Geopolitics* 14, no. 2 (2009): 325.

have received little criticism, politically or financially. The California Public Employees' Retirement System (CalPERS), established in 1932, is in fact very similar to SWFs in terms of both the magnitude and structure of its portfolio. CalPERS held about $205.7 billion worth of assets as of 20 January 2010. In 1999, the board of directors of CalPERS was given absolute and exclusive authority over the administration and management of the pension fund. The fund has a diverse portfolio both in terms of geography and investment instruments. As of the end of October 2009, over 64 percent of the portfolio consisted of equities (both domestic and international), 24 percent of fixed income assets (domestic and international), and the rest was held in cash, real estate equities, and other instruments.[18]

Another example is the Alaska Permanent Fund Corporation (APFC), established in 1980, which held about $34.7 billion worth of assets as of 21 January 2010.[19] The portfolio of APFC in 2009 consisted of 38 percent equities, 22 percent bonds, 12 percent real estate, and the rest in cash, private equity, and other forms of investment. While APFC's real estate holdings were confined to the United States, its stock holdings as of the end of September 2009, were spread over more than 50 different countries, including China, India, Singapore, Norway, and the Russian Federation.[20] Interestingly, unlike CalPERS, APFC has participated in the International Forum of SWFs. While investment by SWFs has attracted much attention during past years—either from the political or international financial standpoint—international investments by large pension funds have been considered a customary business practice and were not challenged by the target states.

Fourth, the history repeats itself. Today's concerns over SWFs are to some extent comparable to the concerns that both national governments and the international community had at the height of the expansion of multi–national companies (MNCs) in the late 1960s. At the time, many scholars believed that the rise of the new actors undermined nation–states. The opening lines of Vernon's famous book, *Sovereignty at Bay*, capture its tenor very well: "Suddenly, it seems, the sovereign states are feeling naked. Concepts such as sovereignty and national economic strength appear curiously drained of meaning."[21] George Ball, in 1967, predicted that there would be an increased conflict between MNCs and the nation–state, the former being a modern concept evolved to meet the requirements of the modern age and the latter being old–fashioned and inadaptable to the complex needs of the

18   "California Public Employees' Retirement System," http://www.calpers.ca.gov/.
19   "Alaska Permanent Fund Corporation," http://www.apfc.org/home/Content/home/index.cfm.
20   Ibid.
21   Raymond Vernon, *Sovereignty at Bay: The Multinational Spread of U.S. Enterprises*, The Harvard Multinational Enterprise Series (New York: Basic Books, 1971), 3.

present world.[22] Other scholars like Stephen Kobrin, however, argued that neither the end of the nation–states nor compromised sovereignty ever materialized.[23]

The rise of SWFs shows that states are becoming increasingly responsible for the management of their economies. In fact, the revival of the state and its increased intervention in the markets in the wake of the recent financial crisis has already led to a number of fierce debates that may shape future policies in significant ways. Many of the world's largest corporations and financial institutions are now owned or controlled by states. This indicates that we need to review our expectations with respect to the role of states, at least on the economic side. Liberal economists and advocates of the Washington Consensus have argued that governments' involvement in the economy should be minimal but we have already entered a new era that requires a greater degree of state intervention. In addition to governments' bail–out plans and stimulus packages, changes in demography have also necessitated increased state spending because "[a]ging populations will consume ever more public healthcare and ever bigger pensions."[24] To summarize, the rise of the SWFs requires a "paradigm shift" in our approach to international political economy.

One thing is certain and that we have to continuously seek to enhance our understanding of the functioning of SWFs. We need to engage them in further dialogue and the International Forum of SWFs is only the first step in that direction. At the same time, the political concerns regarding the potential negative impacts of SWFs on the recipient states should be reviewed in close conjunction with the potential benefits of their investments. These funds, with their long–term investment approaches can provide low–risk liquidity. As a matter of fact "SWFs could also contribute to greater market efficiency and lower volatility by diversifying the global investor base."[25] Recipient states can direct foreign portfolio investment to specific industries by providing incentives or providing guarantees of protection from legal risks such as expropriation and nationalization. In summary, "state capitalism" should be appreciated or, at the minimum, regarded with less scrutiny. The sooner everyone recognizes and embraces this paradigm shift the smoother would be the transition from the old percept to the new.

Although this study did not support the applicability of the economic statecraft perspective in its traditional form of pursuing power to any of the funds discussed earlier, it does not totally refute the possibility of a fund moving in that direction. The funds studied here were the world's largest in their own class (see Chapter

---

22   George W. Ball, "The Promise of Multinational Corporation," *Fortune* June, no. 75 (1967): 80.

23   Stephen J. Kobrin, "Sovereignty@Bay: Globalization, Multinational Enterprise and the International Political System," in *Oxford Handbook of International Business*, ed. Thomas Brewer and Allan Rugman (Oxford: Oxford University Press, 2001).

24   "Leaders: Stop!," *The Economist*, 23 January 2010.

25   "Sovereign Wealth Funds–a Work Agenda," (International Monetary Fund, 2008), 12-13.

2) and therefore of greater importance than other smaller funds. As was shown, different SWFs are at different stages of maturity, which depend on both the organizational structure of the fund and the political economy of the owner state. Once all conditions are right—i.e., the political system is durable and government is politically stable, the fund has fully developed processes for financial activities, and more importantly, the state is satisfied that it has sufficient financial resources, for its present and future needs—then it may be more likely that a fund will be used by the government as a means of power.

The findings in this book have also underscored the importance of key markers or qualifying questions based on which we can assess the behavior of SWFs in the future.[26] These criteria—including the structure of the fund's governance and its location within the political administration; the structure of the portfolio as well as its geographical diversity—can shed some light on whether the SWFs' behavior is essentially entrepreneurial or, on the other hand, something less salutary. The entrepreneurial funds with the immediate goal of maximizing returns tend to have statutory independence from central banks and other government institutions. These funds typically have a larger portion of their portfolio dedicated to riskier assets, such as equity or real estate, and are usually diversified globally. On the other hand, SWFs with conservative and geographically–limited portfolios tend to be less advanced in terms of entrepreneurial approach. Additionally, funds whose management is not independent of fiscal policy makers are—by the very nature of this dependence—constrained in their efforts toward profit maximization. In summary, the key questions discussed in Chapter 2 can be used when evaluating other funds.

This book is neither the first nor the last book on SWFs, but it was among the first ones to propose a systematic methodology for the micro–level study of these funds within the international political economic framework. It also highlighted the importance of looking at each individual fund (micro–level study) instead of looking at a pool of diverse and distinct funds grouped together. The latter methodology would inevitably result in an oversimplification and, by ignoring the fundamental differences among owner states of SWFs and the funds' structures, would lead to inefficient or even irrelevant policy prescriptions. One thing is certain and that, questions will continue to be raised, which means there are even more reasons to study SWFs in their own right.

Future research could focus on a particular group of SWFs—for instance, non–commodity–based funds (e.g., China Investment Corporation, Australian Future Fund, and Korea Investment Corporation), or sub–national or non–carbohydrate–based funds (e.g., the Social and Economic Stabilization Fund of Chile, the Permanent Wyoming Mineral Trust Fund, and Kiribati's Revenue Equalization Reserve Fund). Another approach for selecting a group of SWFs is by looking at the characteristics of their owner states, for instance, in terms of the type of

---

26   See Chapter 2 for the explanation of methodology and Appendix I for the list of qualifying questions.

the political or economic system. It would also be interesting to see if there is a significant difference between SWFs and major pension funds in terms of investment criteria, management, and rate of return on investment.

With respect to policy on national level, one can look at the ways in which SWFs investment can be directed to industries that the host state favors. In other words, how host states can take advantage of inflow of SWF investment. On international level, one can examine the effectiveness of current financial institutions in dealing with SWFs and addressing concerns of both SWFs owners and host states. Is the International Monetary Fund or the World Trade Organization appropriate bodies to regulate functioning of SWFs, given the fact that the former fosters monetary cooperation and economic growth while the latter is an organization for liberalizing trade? Is there a need for an international investment organization that would "set basic rules and better track the huge and complex flows of cash that now wash around in hedge funds, sovereign wealth funds, banks and financial markets"[27]? There are many questions to be answered and there might not be a straightforward answer to them or a simple prescription for dealing with the SWFs. Further research, however, can reduce concerns about the SWFs investment and foster greater transparency and accountability.

---

27   "Wrestling for Influence; Who Runs the World?," *The Economist*, 5 July 2008.

References

Abdelal, Rawi. "Sovereign Wealth in Abu Dhabi." *Geopolitics* 14, no. 2 (2009): 317–27.

"Alaska Permanent Fund Corporation." http://www.apfc.org/home/Content/home/index.cfm.

Ball, George W. "The Promise of Multinational Corporation." *Fortune* June, no. 75 (1967).

"California Public Employees' Retirement System." http://www.calpers.ca.gov/.

"CNOOC Withdraws Its Bid for Unocal." *Asia Times*, 4 August 2005.

Cohen, Benjamin J. "Sovereign Wealth Funds and National Security: The Great Tradeoff." *International Affairs* 85, no. 4 (2009): 713-31.

Davidson, Christopher M. *The United Arab Emirates: A Study in Survival*, The Middle East in the International System. Boulder, Colo.: Lynne Rienner Publishers, 2005.

Desai, Sumeet. "Darling Says Sovereign Funds Need to Follow Rules." *Reuters*, 19 October 2007.

Dougherty, Carter. "Europe Looks at Controls on State-Owned Investors." *The New York Times*, 13 July 2007.

Egenter, Sven. "Sovereign Wealth Funds Need Rules–SNB's Hildebrand." *Reuters*, 18 December 2007.

Hufbauer, Gary Clyde, Yee Wong, and Ketki Sheth. *US–China Trade Disputes: Rising Tide, Rising Stakes*, Policy Analyses in International Economics 78: Peterson Institute for International Economics, 2006.

Kobrin, Stephen J. "Sovereignty@Bay: Globalization, Multinational Enterprise and the International Political System." In *Oxford Handbook of International Business*, edited by Thomas Brewer and Allan Rugman. Oxford: Oxford University Press, 2001.

"Leaders: Stop!". *The Economist*, 23 January 2010, 11-12.

"Sarkozy Attacks Wealth Funds on Eve of Mideast Trip." *Reuters*, 12 January 2008.

Shemirani, Manda. "Sovereign Wealth Funds: The False Promise of Transparency." *Infinity Journal* 1, no. 5 (2009).

Soanes, Catherine, Sara Hawker, and Julia Elliott. *Paperback Oxford English Dictionary*. 2nd ed. Oxford; New York: Oxford University Press, 2006.

"Sovereign Wealth Funds–a Work Agenda." International Monetary Fund, 2008.

Vernon, Raymond. *Exploring the Global Economy: Emerging Issues in Trade and Investment*. Cambridge, Mass. and Lanham, Md: Center for International Affairs, University Press of America, 1985.

———. *Sovereignty at Bay: The Multinational Spread of U.S. Enterprises*, The Harvard Multinational Enterprise Series. New York: Basic Books, 1971.

"Wrestling for Influence; Who Runs the World?". *The Economist*, 5 July 2008.

Appendix I
Key Theoretical Markers

I. Economic Statecraft II. State Entrepreneurship III. Domestic Compensation	I	II	III
1	There is a close relationship between political leaders and the management of the fund, no independent management	✓		
2	Political leaders refer to the fund as a means of statecraft or foreign policy tool	✓		
3	Fund invests in sensitive industries such as defense	✓		
4	Fund's performance is based on economic principles, fund reacts to movements in the market		✓	✓
5	Fund's management is delegated to partially or wholly to independent or external fund managers		✓	✓
6	State has historically acted as an entrepreneur, established SOEs, or intervened in the economy		✓	
7	Fund's portfolio consists of more risky assets (equities)		✓	
8	State is small, traditionally open, resource–abundant or in general, vulnerable to external shocks			✓
9	State has a low tax basis or the tax system is inefficient			✓
10	Fund is a regular or major source of financing for budgetary purposes			✓

Index

Global Finance Series

Full series list

For Product Safety Concerns and Information please contact our
EU representative GPSR@taylorandfrancis.com Taylor & Francis
Verlag GmbH, Kaufingerstraße 24, 80331 München, Germany